# No Guts No Love

## Burt Gershater

Ed—
Thanks for
carrying No Guts No Love.
The More Love
The better!
Enjoy this stories—
Burt

SACRED PAGES
PUBLISHING

First Edition
Published by
Sacred Pages Publishing
222 North Verde Street
Flagstaff, AZ 86001

To order books: www.burtgershater.com

Printed in the United of America
Produced by Santamaria Design Group
Cover design: Julie Sullivan

ISBN 0-615-2428251495

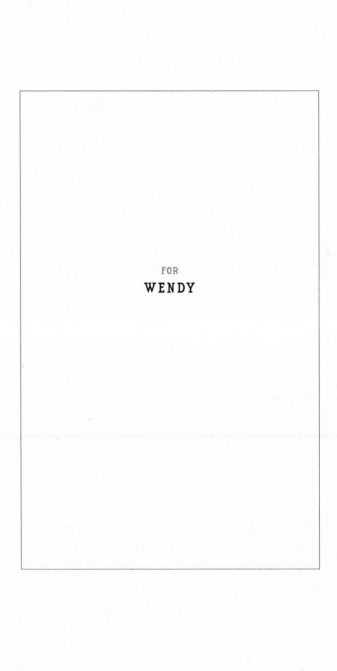

FOR
**WENDY**

# ACKNOWLEDGMENTS

Special thanks to Wendy Weed, my wife, for endless hours of proofing and organizing and then doing it all over again; to Mary Sojourner for keeping me on task and teaching me about the craft of writing; to Tami Gershater, my niece, for her enthusiasm and skillful support; and to Steven Pressfield who as a mentor and guide inspired me to start and complete this book.

I also want to thank the entire cast of family, friends and strangers who fill my life with stories and my heart with love.

# FOREWORD

A student asks a rabbi, "Why do you always answer a question with a question?" "So," replies the rabbi, "how else should I answer a question?"

It's an old joke, I know. I cite it because it's a lot like the way Burt Gershater thinks -- except he answers a question with a story.

Full disclosure: I've known Burt since he was fifteen years old. He was a super-quick point guard with a deadly jump shot and the kind of baseball player who drilled "frozen ropes" over second, one after another. He grew up to be a man you could go to when you were in trouble and he would stand by you and help you find a way out. I can't think of many higher compliments than that.

It's my great pleasure to offer this Foreword to Burt's warm, wise and keenly insightful *No Guts No Love*. I've watched the book evolve through many stages. In a way it started with a series of three-minute TV shorts that Burt did a few years ago for his home-town station in Flagstaff, Arizona. When I saw them for the first time, I thought, "These should be on every station." Burt would talk about fear or love or anger or some other emotion or problem that we all deal with every day. He'd tell a little story and you'd go away feeling like you had actually learned something. But it was more than the stories; it was Burt himself. Burt is a husband and father, a true man of the community. There's something about him that calms you down, that restores sanity, that places difficult times in perspective and helps to steer you straight.

Burt's philosophy appears simple, but the more you delve into it, the deeper it gets. It comes from pain and it comes from love. It's rabbinical in the best sense, like the old stories the Hasids used to tell that delivered courage and guidance in a Zen koan kind of way or like the parables of Jesus. It's no accident that the most profound wisdom often comes to us in the form of a tale or fable. Sometimes people ask me why I write novels. I don't have an answer except to say that I can't figure out how to do it in an essay. It's just the way the material "wants to come out."

*No Guts No Love* is not the conventional "self-help" or "life coach" kind of book. It's Jewish and it's gotten more Jewish as it has evolved. I mean that in the warm, haimisch, tight-family, close-knit-tribe kind of way. It's American, it's Buddhist; there's a bit of sixties in there; there's insight that comes from the football locker room and the corporate board room. There's stuff that could only arise from solitude and from intense pain and dislocation. Each question is answered with a story and each story leads to another question. Burt sent me this e-mail a while ago:

*A rabbi taught me this: if you enter the Torah at precisely the mid-point, the word on the left is <u>inquiry</u> and the word on the right is <u>inquiry</u>.*

Read this book. It answered a few inquiries for me; I think it will for you too.

Steven Pressfield
Los Angeles, 2008

# TABLE OF CONTENTS

Life is hard.

Birth is hard.

It's hard to find your path. It's hard to stay on it when you find it.

It is hard to love and it is hard to live without love.

Not getting what we need is hard. Asking for what we need is hard.

Being told "no" is hard.

It is hard to know if we are being selfish or if we are just taking care of ourselves.

Friendships can be hard.

It is hard to hold on to what is precious.

It is hard to let go of what poisons us.

It is hard to know which is which.

It's hard to speak up. It's hard to listen.

It is hard to grow up.

It is hard to grow old.

Death is hard.

With all that said, our lives can be full of joy, hope, beauty. My Sufi counselor told me, "At the moment of birth, we owe the Creator a debt for the gift of our life".

"What does the Creator want in return?" I asked.

She smiled, "Only to shine as brightly as you can so the Creator has more energy to do the work that needs to be done."

Shining is not just a choice, it is our responsibility. That changes everything!

I have been an individual and family counselor for over thirty years. Here is something I didn't always know: people scheduled appointments with me for only one reason. They wanted more shine in their lives.

Every person who sits with me presents his or her unique story: A difficult marriage. An overbearing boss. A rebellious teenager. An abusive parent. The death of a child. Not enough laughter. Too much debt. Sadness that won't go away. Anger that won't go away.

My clients had lost some or most of their spark and didn't know how to get it back. My job was to help them reclaim it. In my counseling sessions--and my seminars and workshops across the country--this central theme has appeared again and again. It is the same theme that appears to teachers, coaches, mystics, healers, shamans, parents--everyone who is charged with guiding others to their highest potential.

This is it: our job is to shine!

No Guts, No Love is in fact a collection of stories. Being willing to live each story changed my life. As I wrote the stories, their inherent truths began to shine. And as I went back and read and reread them, five key lessons emerged. Each story contains at least one of the lessons.

The five lessons are:

    Nobody is perfect.

    Your teachers are everywhere.

    Honor your friends.

    Commitment is not a feeling.

    Protect what is precious.

Each lesson, when lived, can provide fuel for us to shine! I use the words "when lived" carefully. Anyone can "know" a truth. How often have you heard someone say or have said yourself, "I know that," when what is really meant is, "I'm having trouble living it, but I know it."

A truth does not just reside in words. Truths reside in actions. We live them. We surrender to them. We become them. As we do, we become stronger and shine brighter.

There are five chapters in this book:

    One for each lesson.

    Read the chapter title.

    Take a breath.

    Allow the spirit of the title to enter you.

    Then read the short description of the lesson to follow.

    Take another breath.

    Then enter the stories.

    Repeat with each chapter.

# NOBODY IS PERFECT

Who hasn't screwed up? No one. Then why do we spend so much time and energy on screwups--ours and everyone else's? Paying attention to our imperfections is our culture's number one psycho-spiritual energy drain. And the only thing it does is feed our insatiable appetite for more of the same.

NOBODY IS PERFECT. Accepting that reality does not mean we stop having opinions. It does mean we spend less energy on all of our shortcomings.

None of us lives our life according to some perfect script. We are all, more or less, a work in progress. We let our fear get the best of us. We hurt the people we love. We lie. We fail. We blame. We forget birthdays.

Every day we have many opportunities to practice forgiveness and acceptance and to reap their rewards.

## A BULLFROG NEVER FAILING

Peter Scoppettone moved to my home town, Pleasantville, New York from Pennington, New Jersey in 1956. I was ten and a trouble maker. Peter was no better. Maybe I saw in him a kindred spirit. Maybe both of us were driven by hidden anger that neither of us understood until years later. Even back then our sarcasm was well honed. I can't remember how we began our friendship and I can't recount all the details that solidified it over the next forty-five years. But I do know there were a few incidents that would have torn apart a friendship with less staying power.

I was raised Jewish. Peter was Catholic. I went to religious school on Sunday, studied Hebrew and celebrated the major Jewish holidays. Peter went to church with his family every Sunday and attended religious instruction every Thursday afternoon. He always made the sign of the cross when he passed in front of St. Mary's Catholic Church. The nuns cautioned Peter about having Jewish friends, just as they had warned my girlfriend, Madeline Lewis, she shouldn't kiss any boys at our junior high parties. Neither Peter nor Madeline paid much attention to the nuns. Peter and I made FUN our mutual god.

One slow Saturday night during high school, Peter, Mike Phillippo and I drove to Ottinger's Pond to catch bullfrogs. We never had any intentions of doing anything with them. We were just going to catch a few and throw 'em back. We scanned the water's edge with flashlights until we spotted a frog.

"It's as big as a chicken", Phillippo said. We inched within a few feet and plunged a fishing net over its head. The hardest part was reaching in and grabbing the monster. He was a vicious kicker. Phillippo slipped down the muddy bank up to his crotch, but we scored.

We bagged seven frogs in less than an hour. The night was still young. Our mischievous spirits ached for more action. It was either Scoppettone or Phillippo who suggested we leave a few bullfrogs in two of our arch-enemies' cars.

The first victim was easy. Norman Ellis was a geek and he was also a cop cadet. When we were making out in the woods with our girlfriends, he would shine his light in the car, watch for a while and tell us to get out of there. We drove around until we spotted his baby cop car, dropped a few frogs in the front seat and ran like hell.

Next on our list was Glenn Gornet. Glenn was a star football player and an arrogant jerk. He deserved a few frogs, and he got them. We drove to Foly's Tavern where we knew he was hanging out. It was bullfrog justice.

Everything would have been fine, but Peter, who could rarely contain himself, wasn't done. He took out our last bullfrog, tied a string around its neck and walked it down Main Street, right in front of Foly's Tavern. If Glenn Gornet had come out of the tavern when Peter was walking the frog, and linked us with what was sliming his car, he would have killed us. God must not have been ready to take us that night. We escaped the evening unscathed.

Nighttime brought out more than one devil in us. I can't count all the summer nights we snuck into neighbors' gardens and stuffed our mouths with sweet, juicy tomatoes. We would have had a hard time defending ourselves with the evidence running down our faces, but we never got caught.

And there was the night Peter and I decided to smoke dope for the first time. We didn't have any, but we had an idea where to get some. We searched Peter's beatnik sister's room. Sure enough, we found a full baggie in her dresser. I can't remember how we procured the paper, but I do remember we were unskilled in the art of rolling and smoking a joint. Inhaling was a challenge. We eventually choked down a few hits and forced some smoke into our lungs.

After a few minutes, I asked, "Feel anything yet?"

We didn't really know what we were supposed to be feeling.

"No."

"You?"

"No."

We choked down a few more hits and waited.

"Feel anything yet?"

"No."

"You?"

"No."

An hour passed. Same questions. Same answers. Same nothing. The next day Peter delicately broached the subject with Linda. She howled. "You idiot, that was oregano."

The Scoppettones were *Italian*. Linda loved to cook and oregano is one of the patron saints of Italian kitchens.

And there was the adventure in the Adirondacks--New York State's old mountain range. Peter and I loaded up his dad's '65 Pontiac and drove three hundred miles north to Long Lake. It was a major expedition for us. Six hours, six cokes, six burgers and four pee stops later, we drove into Long Lake Recreation Area.

Our campsite was across the lake. We rented a small rowboat to get us there. It was small rowboat and a very big lake. And the bear we spotted in our campsite was enormous.

If we had known anything about bears, we would have spun our boat around and found a motel. But we didn't. We were men (almost). As we rowed bravely towards camp, the bear scurried into the woods and with trepidation in our hearts and a dull hatchet to protect us, we secured our campsite. It was only mid-afternoon and we were nervous wrecks as we unloaded our gear.

We never left our campsite once for fear of being eaten by that bear. Our only discussions that afternoon were bear related. After a quick dinner of Dinty Moore stew, darkness settled in. We crawled into our tent knowing there would be little sleep. We told stories, laughed and listened for the bear's return. The dull hatchet was always within reach. Sunup finally arrived and two weary campers crept slowly from the tent. We threw our gear back into the boat, pulled hard on the oars and headed back to the suburbs.

The most severe test of our friendship happened in Doc Telstrom's eighth grade music class. Peter and I sat directly in front of Doc's piano. We were the heart and soul of his baritone section, destined to sing in the high school chorus.

One day, we were practicing "A Mighty Fortress is Our God". The second line is "a bulwark never failing". Nobody in our class knew what a bulwark was. But we knew it sounded something like "bullshit". (That's how guys are. We hear cuss words everywhere.)

Doc said, "Let's sing this one more time."

I sang with vigor... "A mighty fortress is our God, a bullshit never failing."

The piano stopped. Doc Telstrom went red-faced. He looked directly at Peter and said, "I'll see you after school, Mr. Scoppettone."

Peter looked at me, hoping I would 'fess up, but I was too scared. Peter took the heat. He went in after school and never ratted on me. He told me later, he didn't rat me out because the whole thing seemed so ridiculous. He couldn't believe what was happening. He was sure Doc would never believe I was the one who sang "a bullshit never failing".

I have talked to Peter many times about that day in Doc's music class. We are still best friends and I still apologize for wimping out that day in music class. Peter has forgiven me. Long ago.

Over four decades have passed since my betrayal of my friend. Now just the mention of "A bulwark never failing..." sends us into hysterical laughter. But I bet if the whole scene were somehow to happen again, Peter would still take the rap, and this time, I'd tell Doc the truth.

## TOMMY RYAN, WHERE ARE YOU?

It was a steamy day at Soldiers and Sailors Field, Pleasantville, New York, in the summer of 1955. I was nine years old, standing in the batter's box and I was terrified. Tommy Ryan was on the pitcher's mound. He stared in to get his sign from the catcher. He was ready to unleash his next pitch.

I was the youngest player in the league. Tommy, thirteen, was throwing the meanest fast ball anyone had seen in Pleasantville for years, maybe forever. We were a classic mismatch that ended the same way every time. Thump! Tommy's blistering heater slamming into the pocket of the catcher's glove. Striiike Threeee! The umpire bellowing (as if the moment needed any more attention).

I was a good baseball player for my age, but I never dreamt of getting a piece of one of Tommy's Ryan's heaters. I wasn't the only one that summer who couldn't hit Tommy Ryan's fast ball. His long, lean frame reared back and in one fluid motion that belied its fierceness, Tommy mowed down batter after batter, leaving most of us shaking our heads and praying that we would face another pitcher our next time up. Anyone but Tommy.

A legend began to take hold that summer at Soldiers and Sailors Field. No one could predict the exact trajectory of Tommy Ryan's athletic career, but we knew we would be following Tommy Ryan's brilliance for many years.

In autumn, he was a silky gladiator on the football field. Magic happened every time he touched the ball. Elusive, unpredictable, graceful and dangerous, he transformed football into ballet. But it was in winter on the hardwood basketball court when Tommy Ryan's athletic majesty was transcendent. By the time Tommy was in seventh grade, no defender could stop him. Opposing coaches came up with new defenses to keep him from scoring. Tommy scored at will.

Give Tommy a ball, any kind of ball, it was beautiful. As the years went on, his legend grew. In those days there was hardly a conversation that didn't include one or more of Tommy's athletic exploits. He was a hero of mythical proportions, but still our neighbor.

That's why I had to write his story, because after Tommy graduated from high school, we stopped hearing about him. And for the next four decades, whenever a few Pleasantville High guys got together, someone would ask the inevitable question, "Whatever happened to Tommy Ryan?" The reminiscing would begin again.

Our most vivid memory was the state championship game against Roosevelt High. Tommy dribbled through the entire Roosevelt team with two minutes left. He drove untouched, past the vaunted players on the bigger and stronger team, not once, but twice. In those final minutes, he sliced through the defensive pressure, punctuating each drive to the basket with an acrobatic leap that floated him past his defenders, underneath the rim, stretching his long arm far out in front of him and then reaching back over his head as he gently placed the ball over the rim and through the net. Eight thousand fans screamed in disbelief.

The final buzzer sounded. The crowd swarmed the court. The Roosevelt players motionless, heads down. The upstart team from a little town of seven thousand had stolen the Southern New York State Class A Championship.

When Tommy left Pleasantville to play basketball at the University of North Carolina, a national hoops powerhouse, we knew we would be following his basketball exploits for years to come. It was inevitable.

That is not what happened. We never heard much about Tommy after he arrived at Chapel Hill in the late summer of 1960. What little news we heard wasn't what we wanted. Tommy wasn't getting much playing time. He was having difficulty adjusting to college life, and it was rumored that he was going to transfer to the University of Massachusetts.

What was going on? He was supposed to be a first team All-American. Lead the Tar Heels to an NCAA championship. Get picked in the first round of the NBA draft.

But that winter after Tommy graduated, when the Pleasantville High basketball team was mired in its worst season in history, there were no Tommy Ryan stories to lift us from our depression. We had reveled in those stories for nearly a decade. When they stopped suddenly, a gnawing sadness and disbelief crept into our lives. We filled the void with replays of Tommy's heroics.

Tommy did transfer to the University of Massachusetts after his freshman year. That alone was hard to swallow. From North Carolina to Massachusetts. What had happened? One Saturday afternoon, as I was flipping though the channels of our black and white TV set, there was Massachusetts playing against some other team. I hunted for Tommy. He wasn't on the floor.

Then the announcer said the words I had been waiting to hear for nearly three years, "Entering the game for Massachusetts, in the guard position, Tommy Ryan." I was beside myself. He was back. I have never watched anything with so much anticipation. And then, within a few minutes, Tommy got beat on the defensive end--and he quickly was taken out of the game. He didn't play much after that and I don't even remember if Massachusetts won or lost that game. I didn't care.

I wanted to see Tommy Ryan win that game. I wanted to see him weave gracefully through the helpless defenders, on national television, and lift the ball up over his head and score, like we had replayed it so many times since that Pleasantville championship. I watched the entire game. I wanted it to happen so badly. What's wrong Tommy? I knew that some day I would be watching you play in the NBA. I was sure of it. All of Pleasantville was sure of it. We would be there, cheering you on.

I never saw Tommy on TV after that one game and I never heard anything else about him or his basketball career. My hopes were dashed on hardwood reality. I was young, just fourteen years old and I hadn't learned about dreams and what can happen to them. Most of us had written Tommy's heroic script and had plotted out his future, but Tommy was playing in his own world, in real gymnasiums against real players, each of them doing their best to live out their own heroic dream.

My brother Howie and I used to play a game when we had nothing else to do. It was called, "Who is This?" One of us would mimic a favorite sports hero and the other one had to guess who it was: Sal "The Barber" Magle from the New York Giants, scratching his two day old beard, sneering in at home plate, looking for his sign from the catcher. Warren Spahn, the great lefty pitcher from the Milwaukee Braves, winding up, lifting his right leg to his nose before releasing the ball. The Boston Celtic's fabled Bob Cousy passing the ball around his body as he floated up to lay in two points.

Invariably as the game went on, one of us would say, "Who is this?" And we could feel it coming. One of us would hold the phantom basketball in our hand, take a few long strides as we dribbled towards the basket, weaving through defensive traffic, then leaping into the air, holding the ball in our outstretched hand, curling it up and over our head and into the basket. We would laugh, conspirators, and then ask the inevitable question for which there was no answer.

We didn't know anything new about Tommy; where he lived, what kind of work he was doing or even about his basketball career after Pleasantville, and it seemed the less we knew about Tommy, the more we needed to retell the old stories. Tommy may have let go of us, but we were not ready to let go of him.

The old gang never stopped asking the question about Tommy. "Have you heard anything about Tommy?" No one had. We had nothing left but to rehash Tommy's two unbelievable shots in the final minutes of the championship game. And four decades later, now nearly in my sixties, the memories and the mystery still live inside me.

A few months ago, I was talking on the phone with Steve Pressfield, a childhood buddy from Pleasantville High. After catching up on our lives, we started talking about the good old days, and just as night follows day, Tommy's name came up. We began to retell the story of The Championship Game.

We had to ask the questions: "What ever happened to his basketball career?" and "Do you have any idea what he did when he stopped playing?" Once again, the answers came back as they always had. No one ever expected to know anything new about Tommy, but it had become our ritual of honor to wonder aloud: what ever happened after the final buzzer in that final game against Roosevelt High? The ritual, in some odd way, served us. We needed the shrouded mystery.

As I was talking to Steve, something new happened. I blurted out, "I am going to contact Tommy and find out what really did happen to his basketball career and what he has been doing since then."

I am still in shock that the words had come out of my mouth. I went online to Classmates.com as soon as I hung up the phone. I typed in Pleasantville High School, Class of 1960. I scrolled down the page. Bingo! Tommy Ryan. Oh my God! This could be the end of the ritual as we knew it. There was sadness interwoven with excitement. I was about to ask Tommy what really happened.

I clicked on Tommy's name and started to type.

*Dear Tommy:*

*You must be wondering, what the hell is Burt Gershater writing me about? Or who is he anyway? I am sure you remember my brother Howie... I was four years younger than you back in '55 when you struck me out every time I faced you at Soldiers and Sailors Field.*

*This what I have been wondering about for the last forty years... I was in junior high when you were playing in and winning the two state regional championships. You were the idol of all of us young basketball players.*

*I did the best I could to follow your basketball career after you graduated from Pleasantville High School. I knew you went to UNC and UMass but to the best of my recollection, you did not achieve the basketball stardom that many of us believed was yours for the taking. I would love to know more about your college playing days and how they impacted your life in the years that followed.*

*I know that this is an odd request, but I would appreciate hearing from you about my wonderings.*
*My best regards,  Burt*

I pushed the send button. I waited three days.

*Dear Burt,*

*I hope you and Howie are doing fine.*

*After red shirting at UMass for a year, I got into the starting lineup after two games into the season. I got into a huge brawl in the UConn game and got the shit kicked out of me. Went to the (foul) line for two, missed both, they rebounded, shot for the win, missed and another melee broke out.*

*Two weeks later I received a severe concussion trapping in a zone press*

11

*against Providence. Was in Intensive Care for four days. Basically ending my
college career. I was unable to finish that season and went home and went to
work. Played industrial ball in White Plains but never college hoops again.*

*My oldest son, Kevin, allowed me the pleasure of reliving my past
as he was a star player at the College of Trenton leading the nation in field
goal percentage (73.5%) in his junior year.*

*I still play pick up basketball in an over-40 format, pitch slo-pitch
softball and can fish with the best of them.*

*I married Carol Farnsworth from my high school class and have
three kids and 3 1/2 grandchildren, all girls.* ... Tommy

That was it!? I felt like a kid who had two bites of his favorite
ice cream sundae and was told he couldn't have the rest. Tommy,
what happened at North Carolina? Why did you leave? A concussion
ended your whole career? Come on, talk to me. As soon as I finished
reading Tommy's reply, I started typing my follow-up:

*Dear Tommy:*

*Thanks for the historical updates...*

*Please indulge me with a few more of my wonderings. What hap-
pened at UNC? The Tar Heels were at the pinnacle of college basketball.
The rumor back in Pleasantville was that you had a hard time disciplining
yourself to college life.*

*How did the glory years at P'ville impact your later life? Was it hard
to live up to the thrill of back-to-back state championships? And what are
you doing these days in the work side of life?*

*Thanks again for your time ... Burt*

I was hoping for more ice cream. An explanation for the unex-
plainable. A few days later Tommy responded...

*Dear Burt:*

*UNC was hit with a point shaving scandal in '60-'61. The NCAA
hit us with severe sanctions for four years. A drastically shortened season
and no tournament play. It didn't seem worth it. So I packed up my bags
and headed up to UMass. In retrospect I should have stayed, but I would
not have the three great kids I have today.*

*You could write my life story and call it Riches to Rags. The glory
days of high school faded quickly as I found there are always bigger, faster,*

*stronger players and you can only be the best you can be by working as hard as you can all of the time.*

*The standing ovation I got in a freshman college game was even a greater thrill than the state championships. I held Jeff Mullins, the nation's future leading scorer, to just 8 points before fouling out. After I sat down, he scored 8 straight and Duke blew us out. So all for naught? ... Tommy*

Where does this leave me and the rest of Tommy's lifelong admirers? We knew his basketball career never attained the heights we were certain it would. We had tracked the roller coaster trajectory of his playing days, only the details had eluded us. Tommy graciously filled in some of the blanks. Some of our questions have been answered, but not all of them. Maybe the most important part of this endeavor has been to finally accept that Tommy was a human being, subject to the basic rules of life. We desperately wanted to know "what went wrong?" Well, maybe nothing "went wrong."

No matter who we are, no matter how high we fly into the rarefied air of the gods, we eventually return to Earth. Some landings are softer than others, but no one escapes Earth's inexorable pull.

Tommy came back to Earth decades ago, but many of us froze him in that celestial orbit where we last glimpsed his grace.

Tommy returned home. Settled down and went to work. He did the regular things that we all have to do. Tommy loves his children and grandchildren, plays a pretty good game of golf--and still gets out on the basketball court on the weekends.

I'd love to watch from the sidelines, sitting next to his grandchildren, enjoying who Tommy Ryan is now. I wouldn't entitle his story *Riches to Rags*. No way. My title is *Tommy Ryan Comes Home*.

## SIOUX ADDITION BLUES

"Hi, I'm Burt Gershater, I'm a volunteer. What's your name?"
"Luke."
"What's your last name, Luke?"
"Warm Water." Luke grinned and walked away. It was two weeks later that I learned his real name was Alvin. Alvin Jumping Elk.

I was a fresh recruit in the War on Poverty assigned to a Sioux Indian community north of Rapid City, South Dakota. College hadn't exactly worked out and I had no interest in fighting in Viet Nam. Lyndon Johnson wanted to create a New Society and he had a plan to end poverty. I wanted a draft deferment--and an escape from the tedium of higher education. It was a match made in heaven.

Four of us were sent to Rapid City in the fall of 1966: Cindy Sutton, Ada Mae White, Herbie Boltenoff and me. Ada Mae had some idea of what we were getting into. She was a Crow Indian from Montana. The rest of us were upper middle-class white kids who didn't have a clue. We were swept up by the idealism of the time: Peace, Love, Equality. The times were changing. Poverty was unnecessary and unfair. We had a dream. Blacks, Whites, Indians and Latinos would stand together in harmony and prosperity. The social order would be turned upside down. We were in the trenches armed with high hopes and few skills.

Ada and Cindy moved into a small house in Rapid. Herbie and I were granted a refurbished shack in Sioux Addition, a hellhole just outside the city limits. Most of the houses had been condemned by the city and trucked in--no running water, few public services, but packs of hungry dogs.

On the day we moved in, our house was robbed. The thieves took a pair of my tennis shoes, my stereo, a few record albums, including The Mamas and The Papas, and the Rolling Stones, but not my coveted Buffy St. Marie. Herbie lost two shirts and a half-empty bottle of after-shave.

Herbie was from Scarsdale, New York, one of the wealthiest communities in the United States. A day didn't pass that Herbie didn't mention the shortcomings of our new community. No shopping. No bagels. Too much wind. When the four of us were issued a dull gray government vehicle, Herbie bought a green '56 Chevy wagon. I think it was his escape plan.

Everyday somebody wanted to borrow money or pick a fight. No loan was ever repaid--and somehow I avoided every invitation to fight. Verne, an alcoholic neighborhood fellow, liked to hang around our house. He was drunk most of the time, but he was a gentle soul. One morning, I couldn't find my glasses. A few nights later I saw Verne slumped over a bowl of chile in the Palace Cafe. He appeared to be wearing my black horn-rimmed glasses. Surprised that someone would steal prescription glasses, I walked into the cafe and said "Verne, are those my glasses?"

He shrugged his shoulders and kept eating.

"Verne, are those my glasses?"

He stopped eating, turned his head slowly and looked at me over the top of my glasses like I was a stranger. The waitress rushed over and told me not to bother her customer. I told her he was wearing my glasses. There was a long silence. Verne finally slurred, "I'll give ya th' glasses in th' alley."

Even I knew the alley wasn't a good place to retrieve glasses. Verne went back to his chile, completely ignoring me. I stood my ground. A few minutes later, Verne succumbed to my silent pressure and handed me the glasses. Either he was too drunk or too humiliated that night, but he never mentioned the incident again. Neither did I.

Smokey and Blacky Byington were hardcore juvenile delinquents, thirteen and fourteen years old. Their family was steeped in alcohol and violence, and they had been in trouble with the law since elementary school. Truancy, fighting, stealing, drinking, smoking, sniffing. They were bad-ass kids on the fast track to prison. Police were at their house every week. School was a joke and their grins warned the world: We live by our own rules and we don't give a shit about anyone else's.

They were wild. In our own way, we were wild too. They offered us a challenge. We offered them a side of life they had never known. For most of the year we played with them, we talked with them, we fed them, and they mostly stayed out of trouble. They learned to trust us and we, them. We were proud to be Volunteers In Service to America as we shined hope into their dark world.

Arley and Wanda Rich lived three houses down from us in Sioux Addition. Arley was a handsome bull of a man--five foot, ten inches tall, a hundred and ninety pounds, all muscle. Wanda was the same height, striking, and as lean as Arley was stout. They were in their mid-to-late twenties, and lived in the biggest house in Sioux Addition.

Arley had a government funded job at the hospital. He and Wanda were wonderful parents to their three children: two boys, Ranson and Leighton, three and four, and an angelic one-year-old daughter, Robin, the pride of Arley's life. The Rich family was making it, steady employment, their own home and a reliable Ford station wagon.

I befriended them a few months after my arrival. On slow days, which most were, I would wait on my front stoop for Arley to come home from work. Around 4:30 in the afternoon, he would turn off the highway onto our dusty street, roll down his window and call out, "Hey VISTA, come on over." I would walk to the big house and watch as he greeted the family.

We spent most evenings together, eating dinner, playing with the children, laughing and telling stories. I watched Arley wrestle with his boys, toss his daughter up into the air and catch her as she squealed with joy. Arley, always laughing, always gentle. We watched the evening news. We huddled together during blinding snowstorms. We talked about our roots, so different from each other. Young, beautiful, strong, successful, Arley and Wanda were almost heroic figures in Sioux Addition.

One day as we rummaged through his storage shed, I uncovered an old wood-burning stove. I asked him why he was keeping it. He replied, "These are good times, but they won't last forever. I'll need that wood stove again." I didn't understand.

As the high plains ushered in frigid winter storms from the arctic, Ada Mae, Cindy, Herbie and I further warmed to our new community. We worked with teens at the Catholic parish. We assisted in a pilot alcoholism recovery program. We volunteered with the Community Action Organization and helped bring running water to Sioux Addition. We handed out U.S. Government surplus food supplies. I played guard on the all-Indian basketball team. In six months we overcame much of the hostility we initially met. Poverty surrounded us but we were feeling good about our place in the community.

Winter turned to spring and spring to summer. We were getting wiser. Herbie and I no longer left our toilet paper in the outhouse. It was always stolen. We stopped having endless conversations with inebriated neighbors. We realized that we were not going to end drinking or poverty in Rapid City.

Late one August evening, two months before our tour would end, after Ada Mae and Cindy had gone to sleep, they were jarred awake by the sound of smashing glass. Smokey and Blacky had broken into the house. Smokey grabbed Ada Mae and pushed her into the bedroom. He told her to stay there. Then he blocked the bedroom door with the living room couch. Ada was locked in. Terrified, she climbed out the tiny bathroom window to get help.

Blacky was angry, maybe because he knew Ada and Cindy would be leaving soon, Ada returning to her reservation, Cindy going back to her affluent life in Wisconson, leaving him and Smokey to the streets. But then Blacky was always angry--the beatings, the hunger, the cold, no one to count on. Whatever the reasons, he was angry that night. And vengeful.

He pulled Cindy from her bed, put a knife to her neck and raped her. Cindy sobbed helplessly. She loved Blacky Byington.

The police picked up Blacky a few hours later. We never saw him again. Cindy left for Wisconsin a few days later, scared and scarred. Ada Mae left too.

Wanda Rich knocked on our door. It was dark. She was alone. She was shaking. "Arley has been gone for a few days drinking. The kids are hungry. Can I borrow some money for groceries?"

I took her to buy food. We didn't talk much. Not much to say. Arley was on a binge. She was taking care of the three kids. Arley hadn't been drinking since we met. Not that I knew. He was solid. Hardworking. He'd be home soon. I thought about the wood stove.

Arley didn't come home. He stayed a few more days. Wanda grew frustrated then angry. She left the children at home with her nephew, Bear King. Bear King flipped out that night. No one knows why. He raped and killed Robin. Word got back to Arley and Wanda. They found their way home. It was morning, there were police everywhere.

Wanda sat in the passenger seat of the Ford wagon while Arley went into the house. He came out carrying a rifle. He told the investigating police he was going to hock it. Get money for flowers. They believed him. Before anyone knew what happened, Arley walked over to Wanda and shot her above the right eyebrow.

I was a pallbearer. Arley, guarded by three deputies, his hands and feet shackled, attended the funeral. I visited him in jail in the weeks that followed and worked with his defense attorney, James Abourezk, trying to piece together the events leading up to that fateful morning. None of the nephews or friends would talk to me. It was better that way.

Arley was charged with second degree murder. An expert witness explained to the jury that Arley acted out of a sudden, uncontrollable rage. The jury agreed and the charge was reduced to manslaughter. Arley served three years.

A few weeks after the funeral--confused, angry, sad and broken--I left for home.

Ada Mae is now living in Crow Agency working for the Public Health Department. Herbie surprised me. He now teaches high school in Great Falls, Montana. One of his courses is Native American History. None of us has heard from Cindy.

I had been trying to reach Arley for years with no luck. Finally, in desperation, I sought James Abourezk, his attorney, on the Internet. I found him. In the intervening years he had served with distinction in the United States Senate. He had long since retired and was back practicing law in Sioux Falls. I called him. He is seventy-three now. He remembered the case clearly and thought justice was served. As a last hope, I asked him if Arley was still alive and if he might know where he is.

"Sure, I see him every once in a while. My son Charles is a lawyer in Rapid City, he might know how to find him."

I thanked Jim for his time. He told me he would send me a copy of his memoirs. I was shaking by now.

I called Charles, told him my story. He gave me Arley's number. I dialed Arley's number. The phone rang.

"Burt!" I heard Arley shout.

Thinking this was some cosmic connection, I blurted out, "How the hell did you know it was me?"

"Caller ID, you idiot."

We laughed and laughed. I couldn't believe I was finally talking to Arley. I cried. I wanted to know everything.

Arley had remarried. Had three more children. He was sixty-six now and had been running heavy equipment for a road construction company for fifteen years. He told me about his brother Wallace and his sister Marletta. They were doing well. I asked about Verne. He had died a long time ago. Drank himself to death. Smokey and Blacky moved to Minnesota. Hadn't heard anything about them.

I asked about his boys. He paused. "The oldest one, Ranson, was mugged and stabbed to death on the street. The younger one, Leighton, died in prison." I found out later, Leighton hung himself.

Arley said some things are just destined to happen. That was then. This is now.

I told him I wanted to see him before it was all over. He said, "Not to worry, if we don't hook up here, we will on the other side."

Postscript: I called his sister, Marletta, after I hung up with Arley. She now heads up a prisoner support group in South Dakota. Her daughter is serving thirty years on a federal drug charge. "She got a bad deal," Marletta says.

A week after I contacted Arley and Marletta, they went to a conference in Sioux Falls. They visited their niece, Tiny, whom they hadn't seen for awhile. Out of the blue, Tiny said, "Hey Arley, I found this old picture of you and some white guy."

Arley and Marletta looked at each other mystified. They looked at the picture. It was a photo of Arley and me thirty-five years ago-- two young buddies, joyful to be together.

## KENNY H.

Honesty was Kenny's highest value. This story is about lying. This story is about truth. My friend Kenny wants it all told.

In the late eighties, Kenny began to think he was drinking too much. He harbored the suspicion for four years. As he sat on the toilet, head throbbing, he heard his own voice, "You have to quit drinking, Kenny."

He didn't listen.

There was plenty of evidence: hangovers, diverticulitis, aspirin to ease the pain. More aspirin.

"How much do you drink?" his doctor asked.

"Never more than three." Kenny hoped it was the right answer.

"Research shows that more than two drinks a night is physically harmful," the doctor said firmly.

"How would he know?" Kenny thought, "The guy hardly drinks and doesn't do drugs." Kenny smoked dope a few times a week. He never missed Thursday at the Wild Blue Yonder--an evening of buddies, booze and pot--a twenty year tradition.

Kenny had been a psychology professor at Fresno City College for thirty-four years. His Intro Psych class was famous. Two hundred students packed into his classroom every semester. Old students stopped him in the street nearly every day to thank him.

"You changed my life."

"Thank you Mr. Hallstone, your honesty touched me."

Kenny had become a legend in Fresno.

Kenny mostly drank beer, three-to-four bottles a night and five-to-six on party nights. Except for Mondays--proof he was in control.

Kenny played tennis three times a week, and jogged three miles on the off days. After every workout he drank a few cold ones. He figured he earned them.

Kenny believed Kenny's drinking was Kenny's business. Didn't hurt his son, didn't hurt his wife--too much. Although, friends always seemed to trump family, and friends always meant beer. He did notice that when he drank, he was meaner to his wife, Gudo.

As the years and beers added up, Kenny couldn't ignore the effects. He had been able to sweat out his hangovers on the tennis court. But that didn't work anymore.

Kenny and Gudo took a ninety day trip to Europe. Kenny drank eighty-nine of the ninety days. Every day, he'd say to himself, "Take this one off, Kenny, no drinking today."

In Sweden, in response to the national alcohol abuse crisis, alcohol wasn't sold on weekends. Kenny stocked up on Friday.

"Kenny," Gudo said, "you're acting like an alcoholic."

"Hey," Kenny snapped, "alcoholics don't drink just three beers."

Friends began talking to him. One of his old buddies said, "You have such a good and wise soul. I hope you won't lose that to alcohol."

Kenny thanked him, but inside he thought, "You nosy son of a bitch. You always were too opinionated."

At a dinner party, Kenny asked another pal why he was paying so much attention to him. "I like to catch you before you zone out by 8:30." Kenny didn't reply. But it registered.

Gudo kept after him about his drinking. She hated it when

Kenny was mean, and she pulled away from him when he rambled on at social gatherings.

In the spring of 1990, a former Intro Psych student, fifteen years sober, came to his office to thank him for loving and accepting her during the most shameful period of her life. "You were the one person who loved me through my embarrassing divorce," she told Kenny.

A light bulb went off in Kenny's head. "Thank you so much," he said, "I may be calling you soon on another matter."

Kenny went to her house the next day. She invited him in. Before they sat down, Kenny said, "Would you take me to an AA meeting?"

"Let's go," she said.

Kenny walked into his first AA meeting, ashamed, and terrified to live without alcohol. Another of his former Psych students was sharing her story. She saw Kenny and thought he was just observing. She told the group she had become so self-centered, she hadn't been able to appreciate the wonderful class she once took from her favorite professor--she pointed at Kenny.

When Kenny returned home, he fell to his knees in humiliation. He prayed, "God help me. I need You. I can't stand the shame of being noticed at that meeting. Now people know. Help me God. Please."

The pain and shame lifted within twelve hours. It was a miracle. Shame this deep would usually last for days. And he would always ease it with a few drinks.

Kenny went to three meetings a week. Monday, Wednesday and Friday at 7:00 AM. He had never awakened that early before, but he liked the group. There was a cross section of people--doctors, lawyers and regular working folks.

Kenny treasured his sobriety. The spirituality of the AA program enriched his life immeasurably. He and Gudo were happier. His diverticulitis subsided. And he went from being a good local tennis player to a nationally ranked doubles player. He stayed sober for ten years.

Then, Kenny started thinking.

"Maybe I'm not really an alcoholic."

"The most I ever drank was five to six beers."

"Six beers wouldn't even get the average AA member started."

"Everyone else has more dramatic 'drunkalogues' than mine."

"Not one person in ten years has asked me to be their sponsor."

"Do they know I'm not a real alcoholic?"

"Maybe, I overreacted."

In Kenny's Psych class he taught a section on Drug and Alcohol Abuse that included alternative treatment models for addiction, some that differed from the AA Twelve Step program. In the AA model, the alcoholic can NEVER drink again--one hundred percent abstinence is at the very core of recovery.

In contrast, The Life Process model says that over-drinking is NOT a biological problem. It's rooted in emotional, environmental and social causes. A person can learn to become a responsible drinker. Kenny, who preferred complex over simplistic thinking, liked this understanding. He liked the label Problem Drinker a lot more than Alcoholic.

There was more "evidence" that led Kenny to doubt his self diagnosis: his family history. For fifty-five years, his father drank enough to be labeled "alcoholic." He was under the influence every night; at least two to three drinks; slurred speech, slight stumbling,wanting to talk--for a change. And, he threw in a good rip-roaring drunk now and then. But, in his last ten years, Kenny's dad limited himself to two drinks a day. Since alcoholism is often a family disease, Kenny logically concluded, "If my dad was able to control his drinking for the last ten years, he must not have been an alcoholic. Therefore, neither am I."

At his next AA meeting, Kenny announced, "When I came to AA, I was drinking regularly, but after serious consideration, I don't think I am an alcoholic." He finished up with, "I won't be back to meetings after today. I love you all."

At the end of the meeting one of his AA friends looked him in the eyes and hugged him. "The best of luck to you, my friend."

Kenny didn't run out and drink right way. His first drink was eighteen months later on New Year's Eve. His son's fiancée Aili, gave him a three ounce glass of champagne. "What the hell," Kenny said, "Happy New Year." He remembered immediately why he liked alcohol so much.

His next drink was five months later at his son's wedding--one margarita.

Kenny's confidence grew. He started drinking wine in the evening. Two glasses. Still, concerned he might be making the wrong decision, Kenny called his AA friend, John. "I've gone back to drinking, John. I've done it consciously with the belief that I am probably not an alcoholic, but I will tell you if I suspect I am drinking too much."

John wished him well, "Time will tell."

Kenny drank for two more years. His club tennis pro stopped drinking during that same time. Kenny told him, "Between you and me, my drinking is an experiment. Three strikes and I'm out. If I have more than three drinks, three times, I have to let it go again."

After his first three strikes, Kenny gave himself three more. He struck out at least four more times. Doubt crept in, but he enjoyed drinking. He read the book, *A Better Way to Drink*, which helps some drinkers drink more reasonably.

Kenny stopped drinking beer, his favorite. He experimented with martinis. He measured them so he wouldn't exceed his three drink limit. He didn't cheat on the measurements but he began to have a half martini more than his quota. A new doubt crept in. Maybe he really was an alcoholic.

Then, Kenny's mom confided in him. On his father's deathbed, the old man had confessed that during monthly trips to his friend's home in Parkfield, he always got stinking drunk. He had planned his last ten years around the trips to Parkfield. He told his secret as he lay dying of liver cancer.

Kenny knew he was a member of an alcoholic family.

The evidence mounted. Kenny realized he was planning his day around the 5:00 PM cocktail hour. There were more four-drink nights. Drinking sapped his energy. Kenny couldn't read in bed before going to sleep. Spirituality and gratitude disappeared. Alcohol was edging out God.

And Kenny missed God.

Kenny went to his friend, John. "Please take to me to a meeting." They went.

My name is Kenny. I am an alcoholic."

He told his story. They listened. They understood. They welcomed him back.

Kenny stopped drinking, but he didn't really want to stop. He had missed God, but he hadn't quite surrendered.

Kenny decided he would not drink in his home town, Fresno, but when he traveled he would. He counted his sobriety days by the days he didn't drink in Fresno. A special approach.

He kept going to meetings but he didn't inform the group of his personal version of the Twelve Step Program.

A few months into the experiment, Kenny and Gudo headed to San Francisco, three hours from Fresno. There would be a stop at a little bar in Fireball, California. The place served a great martini, heavy on the vermouth, with three big olives. Kenny limited himself to one. In San Francisco, there were no limitations.

It took Kenny less than two months to see through his new system. He came clean. He made a full confession to the group.

That was two years ago and Kenny is still sober.

## THAT GUY IS A JERK

Wendy and I had driven twelve hours across the Mohave Desert from Flagstaff. We had finally arrived at the Moonstone Inn in Cambria, California. I had made the reservation months ago. The place didn't seem to be open. The office was closed.

We walked the property looking for someone to check us in. A man walked towards the hotel office. "How can I help you?" he said as he unlocked the door. We followed him in.

"We have a reservation for tonight."

"I don't think so," he said.

I hesitated, then said, "You wanna bet?"

I handed the confirmation paper to the him. I could feel the cocky smile on my face. The Moonstone Hotel Properties logo was printed right on top of my confirmation, and the date was correct.

The owner looked at the paper and handed it back to me. "No, your reservation is at the Blue Dolphin Inn. This is the Moonstone Inn.

"Glad you didn't bet?"

No longer cocky, I pointed to the Moonstone Hotel Properties logo. "It says Moonstone Properties right here."

He shook his head, came around the front desk and headed for the door.

"Where is the Blue Dolphin Inn?" I asked.

He flipped his arm to the left and kept walking.

"Welcome to Cambria," I thought.

Wendy looked at me, "What was that all about?"

"Damned if I know," I said. "That guy is a real jerk."

"Freakin' idiot," I said, still shaking my head.

But it was twilight and the waves were crashing just a few feet away and it was our vacation.

"Let's go find the Blue Dolphin Inn, have some wine and cheese and forget about this," Wendy said.

She was right. Why would I let some jerk spoil all this beauty? But I couldn't let it go.

We drove a quarter-mile down the road, found the Blue Dolphin Inn and checked in. We unpacked our bags and opened the bottle of wine we had bought at Eberle Winery in Paso Robles. Wendy unwrapped some brie cheese. Life was already getting better. We toasted each other. The "idiot inn keeper" faded with every sip of Zinfandel.

As the evening darkened, Wendy and I strolled along the coastal path--happy again. We fell asleep, windows open, to the pounding of the surf.

We awoke refreshed, ready for our drive up Highway 1 to a weekend yoga retreat at Esalen Institute. Before breakfast, I headed out for my ritual morning prayer walk. I took deep breaths and felt deep gratitude as I walked along the rocky coastline path.

My mind was at ease. Then, up ahead, I saw the sign: Moonstone Inn. My mind started to churn but something was different. A good night's sleep and my prayerful state had broadened my perspective on last night's encounter.

In truth, I had been a smart ass last night. "Do you want to bet?" The owner knew we didn't have a reservation. I wanted to take responsibility for my wise guy attitude and apologize. It was the right thing to do.

But as I got closer to the Moonstone Inn, I began to waver. "You don't have to fix everything, Burt, let it go, you're on vacation," I said to myself. I kept walking, temporarily unburdened from my plan to make things right. "Who knows what might happen?" I said to myself. "He could get even more ticked off."

And of course I said, "It wasn't that big a deal anyway." That one usually works for me.

I picked up my pace and continued on my prayer walk. But not for long. I knew what I was doing. I was doing the CHICKEN walk. There are always good reasons to avoid a courageous act. I slowed down, turned around and headed back to the Moonstone Inn.

I entered the office. The owner was behind the desk. He looked up, surprised.

"Hi, I am Burt Gershater, I was here last night. I came back to apologize for being a wise ass. I'm sorry, you didn't need it."

Now he looked more surprised. Neither of us spoke. He broke the silence, "You want to know why I was angry last night?"

"Yeah," I said.

"Since you came in and apologized, I'll tell you."

I was touched by this turn of events.

"I bought this hotel four years ago. It was a dream of mine to own a hotel on the coast. I never planned on getting rich, but I liked the lifestyle here in Cambria."

I nodded.

He continued, "About two years ago a fellow named Dirk Winter, who owns eleven hotels in Cambria and other western communities, named his company Moonstone Properties. Ever since then, my revenue has dropped twenty percent."

"Why?" I asked.

"I spend most of my day talking to people who think they are talking to Moonstone Properties. They run ads in L.A. for rooms starting at forty-five dollars. I can't match that. Ten, twenty calls a day. And people who want to stay here--because their family has vacationed here for years--find out they're booked at one of his hotels. His company has a seventy-two hour cancellation policy. So, the people who want to stay with me, can't. I shook my head. "What can you do?"

"Nothing."

"Nothing?"

"What can I do? I don't think he ever meant to hurt me--but that's what big business can do to a small one. I decided I have to sell."

"Sell, that's your only choice?"

"Yeah, I put it on the market last month. Probably someone will tear down the motel and build three multimillion dollar homes on the property."

There wasn't much I could say except to apologize again for my attitude the night before.

He appreciated it. "I know when one door closes another one opens," he said, "but still, this has been very hard. I thought I would live out my life here in Cambria."

I thanked him for telling his story and wished him the best. We shook hands, and I headed back back to my motel.

# YOUR TEACHERS ARE EVERYWHERE

Parents teach. Children teach. The person ahead of us in the grocery line teaches. Cab drivers teach. Rich people teach poor people, and poor people teach rich people. Patients teach their doctors. Students teach their teachers. Sometimes clients teach their lawyers. Handicapped people teach all the time.

Nature teaches.

Time teaches.

Our body is a teacher.

Every encounter is an opportunity to learn.

Every learning helps us shine.

## BEACH BASKETBALL

My wife needs the ocean. Our three kids are water babies. I'm different. On visits to my mother's home in Laguna Beach, California, Wendy, the kids and I would head straight to the beach.

I walk through the surf for a few minutes, then migrate to the basketball courts on the far end of the beach.

It's instinct. I stand on the sideline and watch the high school and college studs go head to head. The first team to get fifteen points wins, in a battle for the right to stay on the court and face the next team of hungry gladiators.

Pickup basketball rules are basic: When you score, you keep the ball, call your own fouls, and you have to win by two points--the same rules I played by thirty-five years ago at the YMCA in White Plains, New York. Nothing has changed, except that I can't keep up with the young guys anymore. My back and knees ache from years of pounding. Still, I imagine myself giving a quick head fake and slashing to the basket for an uncontested lay up, or hitting the long jumper from the three point line to win the game.

One early morning about eight years ago, my family and I drove to Laguna Beach. During my short walk in the surf, I was already thinking basketball. I headed for the courts. It was too early for the young studs. One older fellow, about my age, was shooting baskets--alone. He was beautiful. Six-foot-five. A deep bronze beach tan, powerful and graceful as he hit shots from every angle.

I watched from the sideline. He didn't notice me. If he did, he didn't let on. I was itching to shoot with him, but too intimidated to ask. He took a long shot, the ball hit the rim and bounced into my hands. "Hey," I blurted out, "can I shoot with you?"

He looked at me and shrugged. "Sure." He didn't seem too thrilled about sharing his morning basketball ritual with a short, slightly overweight, aging wannabe jock.

I joined him.

While my knees and back have kept me from playing competitive ball for at least ten years, I still practice shooting whenever I can. To my amazement, I still shoot with an accuracy that damn near matches my glory days as a high school and college point guard.

I was hot that morning in Laguna Beach. Nearly everything I put up, went in. He shot. I shot. Jumpers. Set shots. Hooks. Lay ups. Left handed. Right handed. Back and forth. I passed the ball to him. He passed it to me. Few words. Our shots did the talking.

After a solid hour of shooting, we took a break. We walked over to a park bench by the water fountain, drank, and started to chat.

"I'm Burt Gershater, thanks for letting me shoot with you."

"I'm Phil Anderson. You got a pretty sweet shot."

I was sure he had played college ball somewhere. He was good. I asked him where he had played.

"Wichita State, in the early sixties."

I told him I played for St. Lawrence University in the mid-sixties.

"I played high school ball right here in Laguna Beach."

"I played just north of New York City."

"I shoot around everyday."

"I am jealous!"

He just grinned.

I looked up and saw Jennie walking toward us. "Hey Dad, we're ready to go."

"I gotta go, Phil," I said. "I hope we can shoot around again next time I come out."

"I hope so, too."

Three years later my family and I returned. Wendy walked in a trance to the water's edge. Jennie dove into the surf, Mat and Jessie played in the sand--and I headed over to the basketball courts.

It was early. I saw a man shooting alone. It looked like Phil. I wasn't sure. The guy was tall and strong, hit from every place on the court and he didn't take notice of me. It had to be Phil.

"Hey," I said, "didn't you play for Wichita State in the early sixties?"

He shook his head and smiled. "I remember. Good to see you again. How's your mom?" He passed me the ball.

We shot for a while.

"Tell me more about your high school team," I asked.

"We won the California State Championship in my junior year. In my senior year our team was put in the next higher division. We had to play against schools with three times our enrollment."

"How did you do?"

"We took it all the way to the last game. Lost in the finals."

I shook my head. "What was your highest scoring game?"

He grinned, "Forty-five points."

"Let's take a little break," I said. We went over to the drinking fountain. "What happened after high school?"

"I got a scholarship to Wichita State. Played my freshman and sophomore years. Had to go home just before my junior year.

"Why?"

"My grandma got sick, multiple sclerosis. She had no one to take care of her. Both my parents died when I was young. Dad when I was a baby, and Mom when I was fifteen. My grandma raised me. So it was my turn to take care of her.

"So, did you ever go back Wichita?" I asked.

"Never did. College basketball was over for me, but I still shoot 'em up every day."

"All right then, let's shoot," I said, "best out of ten foul shots."

Phil stood at the line and fired eight out of ten. I followed him--eight out of ten. We smiled. Playoffs.

He returned to the line. Nine out of ten. My turn. I hit my first eight. The pressure was on. I missed the next one. I took a few deep breaths, aimed and nailed the last one. We both laughed.

The next playoff was from the top of the key. Phil hit seven out of ten. I made him sweat. I sunk the first five, missed the next three, nailed the ninth. My last shot hit the back rim and bounced out. We shook hands.

We shot a few more. And then it was time to get back to my family.

"Come by," Phil said, "the next time you get to Laguna, we'll shoot a few more."

"Count on it." I waved and headed to the car.

I returned the next year. Phil was playing H-0-R-S-E with his buddies.

"Hey, Phil." I called.

"Hey, Arizona." He smiled.

"Come on over," I said, "when you finish the game."

Phil won his game with a hook shot from twenty feet out... standing on the water fountain.

He headed over to the side lines. We shook hands. Phil looked great.

"Good to see you."

"Good to see you, too."

"Just turned sixty last week," he said.

He had the body of a thirty-year-old and the smile of a contented man.

"Let me read you this story I wrote about you," I said.

"You wrote a story about me?"

"Yeah."

We sat on the park bench, overlooking over the Pacific Ocean. I read him this story.

My mother moved from Laguna last year. I don't get down there anymore. One day I'll go back, early in the morning and find Phil--shooting on the beach, alone.

"Hey, can I shoot a few with you?"

## LLOYD SHIPP

I was waiting for John Keegan, my business development coach. John is usually on time--except when he gets too busy and forgets to show. Our appointment was for noon. At twelve-twenty I called him. "Keegan, where are you?"

"Who's this?"

"Gershater. We have a meeting at noon today. You coming?"

"Oh shit, what time is it?"

"Twelve-twenty."

"Oh man, I'll be right over." He hung up.

The truth was, I hadn't followed up on half the assignments he'd given me last month. If he couldn't make it, it would be all right with me.

The phone rang. "Burt, I can't make it. I've got too much going on. I don't think I can be your coach anymore. I'm maxed out. Sorry, man."

"That's OK, I'll see you around."

Usually I get bummed at times like this. "What am I going to do without a coach? Keegan doesn't like me. He knows I didn't do those assignments."

But this time, I just thought, "God must have something else in mind for me today."

I headed home in my car for lunch and was at the stop light on the corner of San Francisco and Columbus when my eyes were drawn to an old black man across the street. He was hunched over, slowly walking north. The light was long. I watched for what seemed like half an hour.

The man took a few slow steps, stopped, straightened up, winced, held his back, wiped his forehead and started out again. He took a few more steps, rested, held his back, wiped his forehead, winced, put his head down and kept going.

"I'm giving that guy a ride," flashed in my brain. "Hang on," I thought, "I don't know him, besides, I am heading home to write another story."

The light turned green. I pulled ahead--slowly. When I was right next to him, I rolled down the window. "You want a ride?"

He turned. His eyes widened. He paused. "Where are you going?" he asked.

"Anywhere you want to go."

He thought a little. "Sure."

The man climbed into my car and buckled his seat belt.

"I'm Burt Gershater."

"Lloyd. Lloyd Shipp, thanks for the ride."

We shook hands as warmly as if we were old friends.

Lloyd Shipp was a handsome man, five-foot-six, with a big smile. He wore a baseball cap, and he carried a small satchel.

"Where are you headed?" I asked.

"Up to the Summit Center, the doctors' place. Got to cancel a few appointments."

It was a quarter-mile up the road. I pulled into the Summit Center lot, parked the car, turned off the engine. Lloyd climbed out of the passenger side. I got out. His face was quizzical. "You got business here too?"

"No, I'm just here with you."

Lloyd just shook his head and smiled. "OK."

We went to the first desk at the MRI office. "I want to cancel my appointment for June 23," Lloyd said.

"Do you want to reschedule?"

"No," he shook his head, "not now, maybe later."

The receptionist saw me standing next to Lloyd. "Can I help you, sir?"

"No thanks," I said, "I'm Lloyd's driver."

Lloyd looked at me, shook his head and smiled again.

We left the MRI office and took the elevator upstairs, where Lloyd canceled two more appointments, one with the physical therapist, and one with the orthopedic surgeon.

With the business behind us, we headed back to the elevator. On the way, we spotted some coffee dispensers. We filled our cups and sat down in the lobby.

"Why did you cancel all those appointments?" I asked.

"They aren't doing me much good," he said.

I was quiet.

"I have to pay what Medicare doesn't. I don't want to get in any more debt. Right now I'm living on my Social Security disability check."

"How come," I asked, "you didn't just cancel the appointments by phone?"

He looked at me sheepishly. "Don't have a telephone."

"Couldn't you borrow one?"

"I don't like to borrow stuff."

We sipped our free coffee.

"You know, Burt," Lloyd said, "I'm going to turn sixty-five next October. I figure I hurt my back when I was pulling those bleachers in and out when I was a janitor at the high school. And all that mopping too. That was probably it."

"How long have you been in Flagstaff?"

"I moved here twenty-six years ago from Rochester, New York," he said. "I lived in the projects--had a lot of fun back then. We played basketball and baseball all the time."

"I grew up just north of New York City," I said, "played basketball and baseball too--moved to Flagstaff thirty-five years ago."

We started to talk old-time sports: Dolph Shayes, from the Syracuse Nationals, with the deadly two-handed set shot. Willie Mays, Mickey Mantle and Duke Snyder.

We reminisced about Jack Twyman and Maurice Stokes, two stars on the Rochester Royals. They both grew up in Pittsburgh, Pennsylvania. They were of different races, went to different high schools but played together on the city playgrounds. After high school they went on to star at different colleges, Stokes to St. Francis College and Twyman to the University of Cincinnati.

"That Maurice," Lloyd said, "he was one of the best forwards in the NBA. He could have been the best."

We both remembered how in the final game of the regular season, in his third year as a pro, Maurice fell to the floor fighting for a loose ball, hit his head and was knocked unconscious. A few days later, he collapsed in Twyman's arms and fell into a coma. His mind came back, but his speech was impaired and he was permanently paralyzed.

Lloyd shook his head. "How about that Jack Twyman?" he said quietly.

Twyman became Maurice's legal guardian. He started an annual star-studded exhibition game at Kutchers Catskill Resort in his honor which funded the Maurice Stokes Foundation to help defray his medical expenses. Though Maurice died in 1970, Lloyd and I talked about that friendship as if it happened last year.

We told stories and sipped coffee for almost an hour, then I offered Lloyd a ride back home.

We drove over Cedar Hill--still talking--to the east side of town, and a small cement block apartment complex. I pulled into a parking space thinking I'd drop him off and head back home.

"Come on in," Lloyd offered.

"Sure."

Lloyd's two bedroom apartment was immaculate. "I've been here three years, pay four hundred dollars a month."

"Let me show you my pride and joy." He led me to one of the bedrooms and opened the door. Stacks of long playing records lined the walls: Smokey Robinson, The Supremes, The Platters, Gladys Knight, Dionne Warwick, Willie Nelson, Johnny Mathis, Teddy Pendergast, Marvin Gaye...

"I've been collecting them for years. Paid only a few bucks for each one." Lloyd beamed.

He offered me a chair in the living room. He took one in the kitchen.

"Can I get you some cold water?" he said.

"I'd love some."

Lloyd opened the refrigerator and handed me a Sprite bottle filled with water. He sat down and lit a cigarette.

"You know Mike Bibby," he asked. "He and I became friends when I was a janitor at Flag High. He used to come up from Tucson for a summer basketball tournament and we become good friends."

Anybody who knows basketball knows Mike Bibby. Mike was the three-time Arizona High School Player of the Year. He went on to lead the Arizona Wildcats to a NCAA championship in 1997 and was a first team All-American. Now he is one of the best point guards in the National Basketball Association.

"When he graduated from Shadow Mountain High School," Lloyd said, "I was invited to his graduation. I went down to Tucson with enough money to stay in a motel, but Mike insisted I stay at their house."

"Let me show you my scrapbook."

Lloyd pulled it from his bookshelf and sat down next to me and opened the photo album.

There was Mike Bibby, page after page.

"And check this out." Lloyd went to the back room and returned with a hat. He showed me the front, McDonald's High School All-American. Flipped it around. There it was, BIBBY, embroidered on the back.

It was getting late.

"I gotta head out."

"Hang on, I've got something for you."

He handed me a book.

"Friday Night Lights. It's about a high school football team in Texas."

"Hey, thanks," I said.

"Take your time," Lloyd Shipp said. "It's good. Come back and visit sometime."

"I will."

## ACHY JOINTS

My dad was an incurable jock. He died playing tennis at eighty-two, crumpling to the asphalt as he waited to return serve. His doubles partner told me they were winning five games to three and Dad never stopped smiling as the paramedics tried to revive him.

Dad competed in everything when he was young--football, basketball, baseball, handball, stickball, diving, gymnastics. He won the Best Athlete Contest at Spire High School in Brooklyn, New York when he was only sixteen years old, five-foot-six and a tad under a hundred and thirty pounds. He whupped some big guys and he always loved to tell the story.

Years later, after he escaped the poverty of his Russian immigrant community, he took up more middle class sports: golf, tennis and skiing.

When I was young, Dad did an exercise routine every morning as he waited for the Chock Full' O' Nuts to percolate on our electric stove.

Knee bends, arm circles, head rotations, shoulder shrugs, jumping jacks, leg lifts, sit-ups, fingertip pushups. He even contorted his face to stretch his facial muscles. Then he'd go for a brisk two mile walk up our country road. At least five days a week he played tennis, handball or golf.

Dad's devotion to athletics didn't come without a price tag. Invariably he was rehabilitating from one sports injury or another. A torn cartilage from football. A detached retina from handball. Multiple broken fingers. Severe and chronic back pain. An assortment of pulled and strained muscles. Sprained ankles and twisted knees. Tennis elbow.

As he got older he suffered from arthritis. He put bags of frozen peas on his knees after every tennis match. Finally, he could no longer play two days in a row, but that didn't stop him from driving his golf cart to the tennis courts on his off days to watch his buddies play.

My dad never pushed me into sports, but I inherited his jock genes. I played everything, just like him. High school baseball, tennis and basketball. College basketball and tennis. Now, at nearly sixty, I still get out at least five days a week to get my athletic fix. No more basketball or tennis. The quick starts and stops hurt my knees too much. But I cross country ski, hike alpine and desert mountains, rock climb, roller blade and still run stadium stairs.

I, too, have had to deal with injuries. Every part of my body has been bruised, broken, strained or inflamed. Neck, back, shoulders, fingers, eyes, ribs, knees, ankles, heels and toes.

I am luckier than my dad. These days there is the highly developed field of sports medicine. We have more professionals, knowledge and techniques to help prevent and heal our injuries. There are doctors who specialize just in sports medicine and chiropractors to readjust us back to the playing field. There are massage therapists and body workers to take the kinks out of our overused muscles. And there are ten schools of yoga, each with their own slant on physical health and spiritual enlightenment.

I've used most of them. Alone and in combinations. But they all take time. I am a busy professional. And I'm a guy.

So I mostly push through the pain--just like my dad.

For six months, my shoulders had ached, ever since I started roller blading using my cross-country ski poles. I jammed both poles into asphalt thousands of times every workout. I developed sharp pain in both shoulders. Whenever I moved into the wrong position, I grimaced. It got to where I couldn't sleep on my left side. And sometimes just grabbing a fork the wrong way would make me yelp.

I've had shoulder problems before. A few years ago I had rotator cuff surgery on my right shoulder from straining it on a hard rock climb and from, you guessed it, poling on asphalt roads. But I've learned how to treat it. I iced both shoulders with a high tech powder, frozen in sealed bags (the modern version of frozen peas). I took aspirin three times a day. I rested, but not often. Stretched, but not much. The pain persisted, but I continued to train, jamming the ski poles into the street a few times a week.

It was September. Snow would be falling soon and that meant cross-country ski season was fast approaching. Finally, with both shoulders aching too much to train, I succumbed and made an appointment with Shane, my body healer. He looked me over, did some deep muscle tissure work to relieve the compression caused by pounding my shoulder joints day after day and showed me a few yoga stretches to open up space in my shoulder joints. He told me to do the exercises at least five days a week.

A few weeks later at our next session, Shane asked, "Have you been doing the yoga?"

"Not much. I've been pretty busy. Here is what I do already. I do an hour prayer walk every morning. Then I write for an hour or more. I do a cardio workout for another hour. And I have to work! There's not much time left for yoga."

Shane listened.

A few weeks later.
"How are your shoulders?"
"Still sore."

"Are you doing the yoga?"

" I did it a few times. My schedule is still crazy."

Shane gently explained that my health was in my own hands. I couldn't disagree.

"I'll do better," I said obediently.


A month later.

"How are your shoulders?"

"About the same."

"You been doing the yoga?" He knew the answer.

"Not really," I answered lamely.

Shane reached into his arsenal of coercive tools. "Burt, let me tell you the way it is. You can either inconvenience yourself by adding yoga to your busy schedule or you can inconvenience yourself with shoulder pain for the rest of your life. Those are your ONLY choices!"

God spoke to me that day.

For the next two months, I set aside time for yoga. Three to five minutes. Five to six days a week. I never missed a day. I moved through the yoga positions quickly to limit their impact on my busy schedule. And my shoulders felt a little better. Very little.

When I'd see Shane I'd say, "I've been doing my yoga--three to five minutes every day."

Shane seemed pleased that I was creating a new habit--a short one--but a habit nonetheless.

A few weeks later, Shane told me, "You have to get your yoga up to at least fifteen minutes to get significant benefit."

I said, "Shane, when you told me I only had two choices: either inconvenience my busy schedule with yoga, or inconvenience my life with pain, that worked! Would you come up with something to get me up to fifteen minutes a day?"

He grinned as we started our training session.

"Burt, why don't you warm up?"

I began. Holding an eight pound rubber ball, I twisted my torso gently side to side. Then I moved into a fluid over-the-head arm motion.

About three to five minutes into my session, Shane said, "OK, that's enough for today. Let's go home."

Usually our sessions lasted an hour and a half.

I was puzzled and continued my warm ups.

Shane said firmly, "That's three to five minutes. See you in a few weeks."

God spoke again!

I got it. I increased my yoga to fifteen minutes, five to six times a week and my shoulders started to feel better.

At my most recent session, I knew what was coming. "Get it up to thirty minutes," Shane said.

Now I do thirty minutes of yoga, six to seven times a week. It slows me down. My muscles relax. And my shoulders don't hurt anymore.

I wish Dad had met Shane.

## WHO IS THE TEACHER?

I was mean to my son when he was young. Mathew was a good boy. I screamed at him, picked him up, shook him. I squeezed his shoulder until pain buckled his legs.

My daughters, Jennie and Jessie were spared most of my rages. The worst were saved for Mathew. I have theories about all this. But for now, I just want to acknowledge what I did.

This story comes from the days before peace was made.

One evening when Mathew was five, he came to me and said, "Daddy, you aren't going to tuck me in tonight, are you?"

"Daddy, you aren't going to tuck me in tonight?" I repeated Mathew's words to myself. Mathew's bases were covered. If I had told him, "No, I'm not going to tuck you in tonight," he would have been able to hide most of his sadness as he tucked himself into bed. But his tears, shed or not, would have been felt by both of us.

At that time in my counseling career, I was teaching assertiveness classes. When Mathew came to me that evening, I paid close attention to the phrasing of his request. I thought this would be a good opportunity to teach him a lesson about asking for what you want more directly.

"Mathew, I know it's hard to ask Daddy to tuck you in. Could you say to me, 'Would you tuck me in tonight, Daddy?'"

Looking back now, I see that I was asking my five-year-old boy to act like a man, even though for much of his life, I had acted like a child. Mathew was quiet for a while. Tears welled up in his eyes. If he exposed his true desire, my rejection was a possibility.

Mathew trembled, on the threshold of my unknown response to his direct request. Mustering up his usual courage, he finally said to me, "Daddy, would you tuck me in tonight?"

I didn't make him wait. "Yes I will, Mathew. It's harder to ask that way, isn't it?" He nodded "yes". Tears rolled down his red cheeks.

We went to his room. I helped him get ready for bed, tucked him in, then I lay next to him and put my arm around him. I started to think about my own childhood and I couldn't remember my dad ever tucking me into bed. "Mathew," I said, "you know, I can't remember my daddy tucking me into bed."

Mat rolled over, looked at me and said, "Did you ever ask him?"

I couldn't speak. My son struck me to the bone. That night Mathew was my teacher. I had always been afraid to ask for what I wanted, muted by the specter of rejection.

I hugged Mathew, kissed him on the forehead and I have never forgotten the words he spoke to me that night.

## I AM BEAUTIFUL

"You are beautiful," Karen said to me.

I froze.

We sat in a circle, fifteen of us, students in a Gestalt Therapy training group. I was a few months shy of my thirtieth birthday. My first child was due in two months.

That day our trainer was the elf-like Bob Martin. He was a genius.

Bob had just led me for nearly an hour through layers of ancient fear. He'd helped me expose my tender heart. In that hour I was afraid. I raged. I laughed. I told my story. I sobbed, and learned to be less protected and more alive.

When I was finished, I sat peacefully and listened to feedback from my fellow students, with no idea of what was coming.

I had begun this course of study a few years earlier at Esalen Institute, in Big Sur, California. Esalen Institute is the mecca for personal growth seminars. It is perched on a bluff overlooking the Pacific Ocean and seekers from around the globe come to learn.

There is yoga, meditation, group therapy, drumming, organic gardening, dance, chanting, body work, hot baths and more. Participants recharge in weekend or week-long workshops with many themes: *Dare to Say Yes to the Givens of Life, Mindfulness and Heartfulness, Awakening the Mind: Mastering the Power of Your Brain Waves, Vinyasakrama Yoga, The Soul of the African Drum.* There are more than four hundred workshops every year.

In my first visit to Esalen in 1973, I could tell it was the place for me.

In my second trip, I had my first therapy breakthrough.

Frank Rubenfeld, a long haired hippie-type fellow, was our leader. His first words to us were, "Therapy is a hero's journey. You begin by stepping off the shore, alone, and begin to face your demons. This is not an activity for the weak of heart."

I paid six-hundred dollars for five days of intensive Gestalt Therapy--a ton of money for a graduate student in the mid-seventies. The format was simple: We sat on the floor in a circle. The leader said "Who wants to work?" Usually a silence followed, as participants weighed their desire to shed a layer of psychic sludge against their fear of exposing the same.

If you had the inclination and the courage, you said, "I'd like to work on something", then moved to the center of the circle (the Hot Seat), face-to-face with the therapist.

And you would cast off.

After three days at the Esalen Gestalt Intensive, I hadn't said a single word. I balked at every opportunity to "work". I was too scared. But I was acutely aware that my opportunity to get my money's worth was slipping away. On the fourth day, emboldened by my desire to not throw away my hard-earned money, I finally spoke up.

"I'd like to work on something but I am too scared to say anything," I finally blurted out.

Frank looked at me and smiled--a smile that seemed to say he knew something I didn't know. "I'll bet you get at least this much satisfaction out of being so scared." He held up his hand and put his thumb and forefinger about a sixteenth of an inch apart.

Frank said, "I want you to go from person to person and tell each of them what you get out of being so scared."

I moved away from my place in the circle and sat in front of the first person and began my journey. "As long as I am scared...I don't have to do anything scary."

I moved to the next person. "As long as I am scared...someone will help me out."

Then the next person. "As long as I am scared...I can hide."

One more, "As long as I am scared...I have an excuse."

I got it.

Fast forward.

"You are beautiful."

Bob watched me freeze. "You had a little trouble with that," he said.

I looked up. Bob was still with me.

"I did."

Bob paused. He waited. I sat with my feelings.

When Bob saw I was ready, he said, "Burt, say to the group, 'I am beautiful'."

I saw it coming, but still I cried. A cry mixed with a soft laugh. Because I knew it was time.

I looked out at my friends. Steadied myself. Took in a breath. I opened my mouth to say the words. My throat tightened. Nothing came out. Just a choking sound. I tried a few more times. Nothing.

Out of frustration--and for a touch of comic relief--I blurted it out.

"I am beautiful." We all laughed. It didn't count. I knew it. They knew it. Bob knew it.

It was time, but this baby wasn't coming easily.

Bob knew my first child was due in two months. "I want you to imagine your child in front of you. Tell your child."

The gig was up. I bawled. If I couldn't say it to myself, how would my child learn to say it? This wasn't only about me anymore. Now, I was ready.

I saw my little baby lying in front of me. "I am beautiful," I said. And again, "I am beautiful, little one."

And with that, I came home.

Two months later, my wife Mary Lou and I drove to the hospital. After twenty-four hours of hard labor, Jennie was in our arms. I looked into her dark eyes. "I am beautiful," I said.

I first told this story to Jennie when she was three years old. She always loved hearing it and I liked telling her. My daughter Jennie has been able to say "I am beautiful" all of her life.

## STANLEY ASHE

Mr. Ashe was my favorite teacher of all time. I loved him. Everybody loved him. He taught junior high English.

He left teaching abruptly in the fall of our eighth grade year. He walked into class and told us he was leaving. Going into business, selling plastic signs with a friend. I was numb. We were all numb. Plastic signs. Mr. Ashe, gone.

Mr. Ashe was the first teacher who I knew saw something in me. A spark. Something. Maybe it was the way he talked to me, the way he laughed at my jokes. Maybe it was simply a connection between two people--two guys. He was my first male teacher. But I bet it had nothing to do with teacher-student. We just hit it off.

It was the late fifties, a few years post-Sputnik, and America was scared. They wanted to insure that the smartest and most talented students would get special academic attention. We were behind in the space race, and President Eisenhower got the word out to America's schools. WE NEED SCIENTISTS AND MATHEMATICIANS!! School districts responded by separating each grade level into groups based on I.Q. tests and past academic performance.

I was placed in the Average Class. Not the smartest, but not the dumbest. Not that any of it really meant anything anyway. Henry DeNero was in the slowest class. He graduated tenth out of three hundred seniors, went to Amherst College, one of the best colleges in the east, and became a huge success in corporate America. Paul Mocha was also in the slowest class. He got kicked out of high school for telling the principal to fuck off. Paul was our class's first millionaire. But America was playing the odds, and the odds makers said we would win the space race if we preselected our brain trust.

I didn't like being in the average class. But the truth is that in the classroom, I thought of myself as average, at best.

In other ways, I was definitely not average. I was funny. Very funny. All I'd have to do is walk into class and people laughed. I was cute. I was voted "cutest smile" in eighth grade and my senior year. I was one of the best athletes and I won every school election by a landslide. AND the girls liked me.

On my report cards, I got mostly B's, a few C's and an occasional A. My grades for behavior and effort were often ID-- Improvement Desired.

It was not unusual for me be sent to the principal's office for bad behavior, even in elementary school.

I always got an A in physical education.

Mr. Ashe was Pleasantville High School's varsity basketball coach. He had graduated from Central Connecticut University four years earlier. He had been the leading scorer on the basketball team in his senior year, averaging about 18 points a game. Mr. Ashe was six-foot-four, handsome and a phenomenal teacher.

I'm pretty sure I was Mr. Ashe's favorite, and not just in the classroom. Early on he noticed I was a good basketball player. He took extra time to coach my friend Roy Colsey and me after school.

I had never had a real basketball coach before. Mr. Ashe taught us offense. He had us dribbling with both hands through a line of folding chairs. Taking shots from every angle on the court. He taught us two handed passes. Bounce passes.

He taught us defense. He showed us how to get low. How to slide our feet to stay in front of the offensive player. How to cut off the angle to the basket. The same drills. Over and over. Tuesday after Tuesday. We got better.

We thought we were hot stuff. The varsity basketball coach working with seventh graders.

One time after practice, Mr. Ashe taught me how to tie a Windsor necktie knot. He had a special trick. I still use that trick, and taught it to my son Mat years later.

Mr. Ashe came to my Bar Mitzvah when I turned thirteen in June of seventh grade. He presented me with my first Webster's College dictionary. I used it all through high school, college and graduate school.

But the most amazing thing about Mr. Ashe was that he made English grammar exciting. Like a coach. He would write a complex sentence on the chalkboard. "What's the subject?" he asked. "What's the predicate?" "Is that a phrase or a clause?" "Why?" "Does it modify the subject or the predicate?" "Is it a prepositional phrase?" "What's the object of the preposition?" "Is that a verb or an adverb?" "Why?" He drilled us everyday. Over and over. Every day.

I loved it and I still know my grammar.

Despite Mr. Ashe, I still thought of myself as barely an average student. And to make matters worse, my parents expected me to do better than I believed I could. This led me down a path I'm not proud of: I often cheated to make better grades. In French class, math class and even in English class, I'd bring in cheat sheets. Write on my hand. Or take a peek at the paper on the desk next to me.

Mr. Ashe gave us an assignment. We had to write a short story. I didn't think I could do it. I didn't even try to do it. I went home and looked through my brother's old English papers, hoping to find one that would match what I needed. I found one. I didn't even re-type it. I just erased the teacher's corrections and handed it in.

Mr. Ashe handed back our assignments a few days later. Everybody's but mine. He held my paper in his hand. "I'd like to read you Burt's story," he said. I shuddered. Mr. Ashe read beautifully. When he finished, he handed "my" story back to me. He'd written on the top in red: 'A'--Very Good Work!"

I exhaled and thought "I dodged a bullet."

Over the years, I've thought often about that moment. Mr. Ashe knew. He had to know.

That winter I went to every Pleasantville High home basketball game and most of the away games. Mr. Ashe molded the young team. There were no seniors. They were naturals on offensive, but Mr. Ashe taught them defense--a tough man-to-man defense that had opponents struggling to get off a shot. He taught freshman guard, Jeddy Devine, to shoot a deceptive two-handed set shot from the top of the key that stretched defenses and created more room for juniors Tommy Ryan and Bobby TeCarr to score inside.

Mr. Ashe knew he had something special from his first practice in October. But it was no cake walk. Tommy Ryan, one of the junior phenoms was hot--and Tommy knew it. He was used to doing whatever he wanted. Mr. Ashe had other ideas. During one practice early in the season, Tommy was off doing his thing when the team was running a drill. Mr. Ashe benched him for most of the next game. Tommy got the message.

After a 14-5 regular season, Pleasantville won the Class B Southern New York State Basketball Championship. They beat Harrison High in the championship game. Tommy Ryan was one of the brightest stars and Peter Scoppettone and I were in the stands, screaming our heads off for Pleasantville High and our favorite teacher.

Mr. Ashe made seventh grade the best school year of my life. Nearly everyone felt the same way, and eighth grade was going to be even better. I was going to play on the junior high basketball team. Madeline Lewis was still my girlfriend, and I was the president of the student government. And, Mr. Ashe was my English teacher again.

Paradise didn't last long. A few weeks into the semester, Mr. Ashe came into class looking more serious than usual. He sat down on the desk. We waited. "I've decided to leave teaching," he said. "I am going into business, my last day will be a week from Friday." We were stunned. Rocked. I didn't want it to be true. I remember helping write a letter, asking him to reconsider, to stay one more year.

But Mr. Ashe had made his decision. I was sad, hurt and angry. And I missed him every day.

I was brutal to his replacement. I made her suffer for my pain. I made her cry every week. She kicked me out of class. Mr. Bucher, the principal, gave me the same lecture every time--something about behaving myself. It never got through. I never got over it that year. But I carried Mr. Ashe inside of me. Just saying his name made me happy. I didn't know where he went. I lost track of him for over forty years.

Four or five years ago, Peter Kuracheck, one of my brother's high school friends now in Tampa, Florida, told me Mr. Ashe also lived in Tampa.

I found the number of Ashe Industries and called.

"Ashe Industries, how can I direct your call?"

"May I speak to Stanley Ashe?"

"May I tell him who is calling"?

"Tell him it is Burt Gershater." I didn't know if he would remember me.

I heard the phone connect to his office and then I heard, "BURT GERSHATER!" It was Mr. Ashe's deep soft voice. He remembered me as though it was yesterday. We talked for nearly an hour. He gave me his home number and his e-mail address. Before we got off the phone he told me he still had the letter our class wrote him. I asked him to fax it to me:

*Dear Mr. Ashe,*
*As you already know, by reactions of the majority of the students, we would really hate to see you go. We are sending this letter in hopes that*

*you might stay. If you have to leave, we understand your position. We as the student body thank you for the good times, good laughs and especially for the many things you taught us. We hope that wherever you go, you should be as well-appreciated as you are here in Pleasantville.*
   *PLEASE RECONSIDER!*

My name was signed first and over a hundred of my eighth grade classmates signed after me.

We continued our telephone calls a few times a year. He told me about Ashe Industries, a multimillion dollar manufacturer and distributor of aluminum building products. His three boys in their forties run the company now. He is proud of that.
   Ten years ago he lost his beloved wife, Rita, to ovarian cancer. "Those were very hard times," he said. He had recently met someone new, Louise, and they were playing bridge tournaments together. "I am starting to be happy again."
   He read my web page and asked about my work. I told him I was writing stories for a book. He asked me to send him a few of them When I finished *Tommy Ryan, Where Are You?*, I sent him a copy. A few days later, he left me a message. "Burt, I read the Tommy Ryan story and I am giving you an A+." I still listen to that message.

I called Stanley last week. I asked him how old he was. Seventy-three," he said. I told him I was turning sixty in a few months and I was almost finished with my first book of stories. "I just have one more story to write." I paused. "It's called *Stanley Ashe*."
   There was a silence. "I don't know if I can take that one," he said.
   "Well, you are going to have to take it," I said. "When we meet in Las Vegas in two weeks, I am going to hand it to you."
   "How will I find you?" I asked.
   "I am staying at Caesar's Palace, I'll be at the blackjack tables."

In fact, Stan was in his room. I called the minute I got in. He answered.
   "Meet me downstairs in fifteen minutes," he said.
   Wendy and I waited in the lobby. We didn't see him. Then we both felt his hands on our shoulders.
   "I figured that was you," he said.

47

Forty-seven years can be a long time.

It wasn't for us.

Sure, Stan was seventy-three and I was sixty. But more than just time had passed during our years apart. We had both lived full lives during those nearly five decades. We sat down for lunch. We started talking right away. The topics didn't matter. Family. Business. Basketball. Children. Teaching. We weren't re-connecting. We'd always been connected. We were filling in details.

I decided that I'd wait awhile before giving Stan the story. I just wanted to talk. And listen.

Wendy and I, Stan and Louise all met for dinner. As we were being seated, I handed Stan a red folder. "Here's the story."

We all chatted. We ordered dinner. As we talked, Stan read.

He closed the folder. "You have to read this," he said to Louise.

She nodded, "I'll read it back in the room, where I can give it my full attention."

The next morning, Wendy and I met Stan, Louise and the family for breakfast.

I met Steven and Nevin, his twin boys and business partners, Steven's girlfriend, Kim, and Stan's two sweet grandchildren, Chelsea and Madison.

We sat down at the table. Louise looked at me. "I read the story last night." She paused. "This story," she said, "is more important than Ashe Industries."

Who's to say?

## STAND BY ME

Wendy and I were in Pike Place Market in Seattle. We ate crab cakes and drank two frozen mugs of local ale. With a slight afternoon ale buzz we wandered past hundreds of booths. We checked out jellies, jams; beef, elk, turkey and buffalo jerky; candy, cheese, pastry, wine and the famous Northwest coffees. We tasted garlic, sausage, bread and smoked fish. We admired the handcrafted lamps. We checked out used books and baseball cards. We were happy, but leg-weary as we headed back to our hotel, a few blocks up the hill.

Our route took us through an alley angling away from the Market. This was not a dingy alley, but an abundantly flowered alley refurbished for strolling and commerce. As we entered, we heard a rich voice singing *Teddy Bear*, an old Elvis Presley hit. The voice rang out between the brick walls.

"I don't wanna be a tiger
'Cause tigers play too rough
I don't wanna be a lion
'Cause lions ain't the kind
You love enough."

We couldn't see the singer. But as we approached the halfway point in the alley, we saw an older black gentleman sitting on a basement windowsill behind a small stairway. He was smiling, strumming and trying to stay warm as he belted out the Elvis tune.

"Baby let me be around you every night
Run your fingers through my hair,
And cuddle me real tight."

We stopped. Not out of courtesy, but to take in our serenader's understated majesty. He finished up with bold guitar strums and the well-remembered closing line:

"Put a chain around my neck
And lead me anywhere
Oh let me be
Your teddy bear."

The five pedestrians in the "audience" stood mesmerized. As his last notes died away, they burst into applause.

He smiled. "Thank you. Thank you."

I reached in my wallet for a few dollars to put in the guitar case he had pulled over his sandal-clad feet for warmth.

He started his next song, *What a Wonderful World (This Would Be)*, a Sam Cooke classic.

"Don't know much about history
Don't know much biology
Don't know much about a science book
Don't know much about the French I took

But I do know that I love you
And I know that if you love me too
What a wonderful world this would be."

More people stopped. Wendy and I didn't move. I was transported back to high school.

"Now I don't claim to be an A student
But I'm tryin' to be
Oh maybe by being an A student, baby,
I can win your love for me."

A homeless couple walked onto the scene. The woman clutched a full garbage bag to her chest; the man's was slung over his shoulder. They were each somewhere between twenty-five and forty. Drugs and the street had taken their toll.

She was shaking. Her cigarette was gripped tight between her lips. When it wasn't, it was gripped tight between her index and middle fingers. He fidgeted and lit up his own cigarette. When they heard the music, they turned to our singer. They moved close--too close, I thought--to the open guitar case which had begun to fill with dollar bills.

They moved in till their feet nearly touched the case. I was sure one of them was about to make a grab and dash. I readied myself to jump in.

But they just stood and listened like the rest of us, enthralled with the sound of this old man's music. The woman moved with the beat and after a few minutes turned to the rest of us, with a huge smile and wide eyes. She pointed to the singer as if to say, "This guy is HOT".

The man abruptly walked away, a herky-jerky walk. He couldn't stay still any longer.

Our singer finished.

"But I do know that I love you
And I know that if you love me too
What a wonderful world this would be."

More people moved forward. They thanked him with dollar bills and an appreciative nods. He thanked every one, tuned his guitar and started the next song, Ben E. King's *Stand by Me*.

The homeless woman was still shaking, but grooving with the music. Our singer's voice pierced the autumn air:

"When the night has come
And the land is dark
And the moon is the only light we'll see
No I won't be afraid, no I won't be afraid
Just as long as you stand, stand by me."

Her partner paced back and forth about twenty yards away. The woman was lost in the music.

"So darlin', darlin', stand by me, oh stand by me
Oh stand, stand by me, stand by me."

The sun was going down, the temperature dropping. Our hotel was around the corner. I wondered where the couple was going to spend the night. The woman swayed with every note. Her lips still gripped the cigarette. The man still jittered.

"If the sky that we look upon
Should tumble and fall
And the mountains should crumble to the sea
I won't cry, I won't cry, no I won't shed a tear
Just as long as you stand by me."

I relaxed. My fear of a robbery was gone. In the next moment, the woman said to herself, "I have to give him some money." She searched in her pants pocket for change. She found a few coins, pulled them out and dropped them in the case. The man, his bag slung over his shoulder, watched from a few yards away. Then he said to everyone or no one, "I need to give him some too." He put down his bag, dug in his pocket, found some coins, walked down to the guitar case and dropped them in. The singer thanked them both and kept singing. Wendy and I wept.

"And darlin', darlin', stand by me, oh stand by me
Oh stand now, stand by me, stand by me
Whenever you're in trouble won't you stand by me
Oh now stand by me
Oh stand by me, stand by me, stand by me."

The man and woman hoisted their bags and moved on up the alleyway. I walked over to the singer, put in a few more dollars and thanked him again.

He nodded and smiled, "Thank you."

Wendy and I headed back to our hotel.

The music followed us up the hill.

# HONOR YOUR FRIENDS

Without friends, then what? Family can be complicated. There is usually a limit to how close you want to get with co-workers. And even our spouse/mate/partner relationship can falter for weeks, months or longer. Friends carry us through. One friend is great. Two are better. And it keeps going. We usually count only one or two as our best friends, but every one brings us joy in a different, irreplaceable way. A best friend can make even our worst times bearable.

## KICK, GLIDE...KICK, GLIDE

Call me wuss. Call me cheap. I don't care. I don't like getting out of bed before the sun comes up in the winter. It's freezing in our bedroom. I'd rather be cold than pay to get warm from electric heat.

I like it cold in the bedroom, but I also like snuggling with my darling. Sometimes this creates a dilemma. The winter activity I enjoy most besides snuggling, is cross country skiing.

Enter my dear friend and tormenter, Dr. Bob Tures. No one calls him Dr. Tures, even though he has a Ph.D. He's Bob.

Bob doesn't like academic elitism, but he does like cross country skiing--and he likes to do it early in the morning. He insists on being on the trail as the last stars fade in the morning sky. I love cross country skiing and I love to cross country ski with Bob. There's the conflict.

Bob and I cross country ski at least four (and sometimes seven) mornings a week--when there is snow in our high desert forest. My alarm goes off at 6:00 AM, Bob arrives promptly at seven, coffee in hand.

Bob, The Animal, has run over 30,000 miles in every kind of weather, including sub-zero Chicago blizzards. When his legs are sore from running, he rides his bike twenty miles on mountain trails. And in the winter he cross-country skis. Before dawn. He has never been late for our ski date.

On ski mornings I roll out of bed after ten minutes of snuggling and wishing I hadn't planned to ski. I stay in the shower until the hot water turns cold. I put on three layers of clothing and eat hot oatmeal. At 7:00 AM, Bob pulls up to the house. We load the skis and head to the forest.

As we drive away, I can almost see the ski track winding through the aspen. I begin to remember once again, why I get out of bed in the dead of winter. I look at Bob and he looks at me. We smile, "Hey brother, it's good to see you."

We slip on our skis in the predawn light. We are out for hours. We ski up steep hills, through aspen groves, through ethereal white trees in an elegant world of pristine snow. We ski across rolling meadows. Morning air stings our cheeks.

Bob leads for a few miles. Then we switch. There is not much talking and hardly any stopping. One of the beauties of cross country skiing is that one ski glides effortlessly after each powerful kick. Kick, glide...kick, glide...kick, glide. Mile after mile, Bob and I follow each other.

Our minds release clutter gathered from over fifty years of living. Kick, glide...kick, glide. Life has been good to Bob and me, but we both have gone through times that made us wonder if we could go on...kick, glide...kick, glide. Every breath is a cloud in the morning light, but we are warm. Kick, glide...kick, glide.

Why did I huddle in bed this morning, afraid of the cold? Kick, glide...kick, glide. Why can't I remember from one bitter morning to the next how I will be calmed?

Kick, glide...kick, glide...

## SAINT ALBERT

If the I.R.S. were to get wind of this essay about my friend Saint Albert, they might want to weigh-in on the story: "Saint Albert? Let us show you his file," the tax cop would say. "He was not charitable with his quarterly income tax payments over the years. It took over twenty years of threatening letters and liberal payment schedules for your Saint Albert to finally pay off his tax debt to the United Stated Treasury Department."

Albert is not listed in their files under Saints, but neither is he listed under Sinners.

It took him over twenty years to make good on his tax debt and I never once heard him complain about the I.R.S.

My dear friend of nearly thirty years did not earn the title of Saint Albert overnight. It was not a unanimous canonization of the pious voting electorate, those unable to see beyond his rarely shaven face, worn out Levi's and eight hundred dollar junker cars.

"Knuckler." That's what Albert's dad used to call him. Knuckler this. Knuckler that. His dad attended only one football game during Albert's entire high school and college career. He always told Albert, "You should be playing baseball, you knuckler."

Rarely has there been a defensive back in the history of college football who, pound for pound, inflicted such bodily pain on opposing running backs as Albert did in his six year college football career. Albert still has a piece of the Northern Arizona University record for most interceptions in one game, a record that has stood for over thirty years. His dad died from a heart attack when he was sixty, and never got around to telling Albert he wasn't a knuckler.

A couple of decades ago, Albert went through one of his separations from his wife. She would tell him regularly that all you care about is your damn handball. And when she wasn't complaining about Albert's handball, she complained he watched too much television or didn't earn enough money.

Albert found a small apartment for himself, not far from the railroad tracks, on the sleepy west end of Flagstaff. He loved this little spot, nestled at the end of a dirt road, in the ponderosa forest. He was a monk out there, secluded from his friends and family in his haven, about a hundred yards from the local athletic club where he played handball every day of the week. Albert's true home was the Flagstaff Athletic Club, and everyone who knew Albert knew it.

Why was it that Albert moved out of their house? Albert realized he needed to be alone to try to make some sense of his marriage "resentmentship." (It would be only after fifteen more years of mutual pummeling, and only after his wife left him when she moved to Florida, would Albert finally called it quits.)

Albert could live in relative peace and quiet in his bungalow in the woods. He could play as much handball and watch as many sports highlights on ESPN as he damned well pleased. His landlords, Jim and Vera, never once asked Albert to turn off the sports channel and they never asked Albert to sign a lease either. Jim must have looked at Albert and seen behind his happy-go-lucky facade, a weary, confused, honest young man who needed shelter.

Albert always wore an endearing smile, even when he was close to tears. Jim knew what Albert's smile meant. Jim had lived a hard life on the railroad for forty years. Jim and Albert agreed on a rental price for the apartment and shook hands. Albert only stayed at his retreat for a month before he went back home. Time doesn't heal all wounds, but it can help you forget how bad things really were--forgetting and smiling are a lot alike. And, Albert missed his boys.

But in those thirty days in the little apartment in the forest, a lifetime friendship began. Albert became Jim and Vera's son. Jim and Vera had their own biological child, Jay, but over the years his visits became more infrequent. As Jim and Vera began the aging spiral, they did their very best to hide infirmities from Jay; and Jay did his very best not to notice that his parents were no longer able to take care of themselves. The family message was, "Everything's just fine, we'll call you next week."

Just as Jim and Vera could tell what Albert needed when he was looking for a place to stay, Albert knew what Jim and Vera needed. They needed a son they could count on. Albert stopped by two or three weekends a month. He took Jim and Vera out to lunch at Furr's and treated them to home style cafeteria meat loaf, mashed potatoes and Million Dollar Pie. When their old refrigerator finally gave out, Albert made sure they got a new one at Sears for a good price. When Vera had to get to the doctor and Jim couldn't drive, Albert made sure she got there on time and stayed with her during the appointment.

When Jay got married in Payson, ninety miles south, Jim couldn't attend because he was no longer able to control his bladder or his bowels. Vera wouldn't leave him. No problem, they sent Albert. And when the day finally came when Jim could no longer live in the apartment, it was Albert who made all of the arrangements with the nursing home. It was Albert who held both of their trembling hands, assuring them that this was the best decision. He welcomed Jim to his new room at the nursing home and later took Vera back home--where she would spend the night and maybe all the rest of her nights without Jim by her side.

Very few people ever know how Albert dedicated himself to Jim and Vera. He doesn't talk about it. But when we spent time together, he would tell me about watching football games with them, about the trips to the hospital and about washing Jim when his old friend wasn't able to get to the bathroom because he couldn't get out of his chair, and didn't know how to ask for help.

Albert took care of more people than Jim and Vera. He saved my life more than once. When my marriage of twenty-two years blew apart and I couldn't eat, sleep or work, Albert was there, night or day. I would panic and call him, " I am going down Albert, I can't handle it."

"I'm on my way."

As soon as I hung up the phone, I could breathe again--Albert would come. Ten minutes later he would appear, unshaven, a capeless super hero with two cups of hot coffee, a Mona Lisa grin and a twinkle in his eyes that conveyed the only thing he had to do in those dark days was take care of me. For three months, he never let me down.

September 9, 2000, ten years later, I was hiking high in the San Francisco Peaks Wilderness with Wendy.

I was getting my legs in shape for a strenuous trip in the Grand Canyon. I noticed I had no energy. I thought it was the flu. I went home and slept for two hours.

Later that evening as I sat in front of my computer, a disquieting sensation began to build under my sternum. A mild discomfort at first, not exactly a pain. It progressed quickly to a low level ache, and the pressure continued to build. It wasn't a kick ass pain. Not even close to kidney stone pain. Much more subtle, but troubling.

I sucked up my masculine pride, found Wendy quilting in her studio and told her what was going on. She took one look at me and said, "Let's go." In less than ten minutes, the emergency room doctor read my EKG and told me I was having a heart attack.

After three days of intensive medical treatment, I was sent home. I was a weakened and scared man. If I had taken a few more minutes deciding to tell Wendy...if Wendy hadn't immediately said, "Let's go"...if the blockage had been just a few inches higher up in the heart...if the shot of liquid plumber they had I.V.'ed into me hadn't busted up the clot...if, if, if...

Wendy slept next to me in the hospital. She never left my side. When we returned home, she was still not ready to leave me alone. But there was a problem. Tuesday night was her painting class. She had been attending painting class religiously for three years. If she was sick on Tuesday, and couldn't make it to work during the day, she still seemed to feel good enough by evening to make it to painting class that night. For Wendy, her creativity is her life.

Wendy called Saint Albert. The next Tuesday night I went to Albert's apartment, and Wendy went to her painting class. I drove to Albert's, my bottle of nitroglycerine in my shirt pocket. He met me at the door with a blanket in his hand and walked me over to his rocking chair, tucked me in and put my feet up on his book table .

He cranked the thermostat up to eighty degrees and turned on the Diamondback's baseball game.

"Are you warm enough?"

"Do you need a blanket for your feet?

"Should I close the door?"

"Is the chair comfortable?"

"Are you sure?"

This was not my old friend Albert. This was Nurse Albert. After he was sure I really was comfortable and the room was warm enough, he made a huge Italian salad, loaded with fresh garlic, a touch of olive oil, a squeeze of lemon and a dash of salt and pepper.

"Is it okay?"

"Does it need anything else?"

"Do you want some more?"

"How do you like that fresh garlic?"

"What would you like to drink?...I've got cranberry juice, tomato juice or cold water?"

"Here, you take the clicker, you're in charge."

Oh my God! Albert has never given up the clicker to anyone. Never.

For the next month of Tuesdays, it was the same routine. Wendy went off to her painting class and I went off to Albert's. He made a big Italian salad and gave me the clicker. Over a year later, Tuesday night is still our night together. I am healthy now and Albert keeps the clicker. Albert doesn't make the Italian salad with fresh garlic, but we always go out to dinner.

Jim died last week. Albert helped Vera with all of the funeral arrangements. Albert even asked Sister Elizabeth from St. Mary's church to say some Catholic prayers at Jim's grave site. Vera wanted it that way. It was Albert who gave Jim's eulogy at the memorial service--and Albert who drove Vera back home. And when Vera is one day laid to rest next to Jim, Albert will be at the grave site saying his final goodbye to her.

## ROBERT S. BREWER

The telephone rang. I answered.

"Burton."

Only one person calls me Burton. Bob Brewer.

"I've got cancer," he said.

"Oh God, Bobby. What is it?"

"Lymphoma, probably from Agent Orange in Nam. I slept on it almost every night for a year." He paused. "There is no history of cancer in my family."

I didn't know what to say. I had never had a call like this. My dear friend. Bobby Brewer. My college roommate.

Bob was the student body president. I was a long haired hippie. When Bob was in ROTC, training, I was studying nonviolent resistance and demonstrating against the war--the war in which he was decorated for bravery. When I played Bob Dylan records in our dorm room, Bob would make a retching sound and scream, "How can you listen to that guy?"

We stayed close over the years, even though we didn't see each other often. When we did see each other, we rarely saw eye to eye. Bob has never voted for a Democrat in a presidential election. I have never voted for a Republican. Bob works harder than anyone I know--sixty to eighty hours a week. I religiously balance my recreation and professional life, almost to a fault. Bob wears a suit and tie everyday. A pair of clean jeans works for me. Bob drives a new Corvette. I drive a four year old Nissan.

But we stayed close over the years. Very close.

I buckled when I heard his news. Then I said, "I am with you, Robert S., every step of the way, we are doing this thing together."

I didn't know quite what I meant. I knew we were doing this thing together. He told me his treatment plan and I told him I'd stay in touch.

I hung up the phone and screamed. Primal fear and rage bellowed from my guts. "No, no, not Bobby, please God, not Bobby." When I stopped sobbing, I felt disoriented and weak. Still, from somewhere deep inside, I felt peace. I would be there for Bobby and we would do this thing together.

The next morning I called his secretary, Linney, got his e-mail address and wrote him this message; "I was just thinking of these words from some of my favorite songs..."

"Just call out my name and I'll be there..."

"Hold your head up high and don't be afraid of the storm..."

"Thank you for being a friend."

"All my lovin', I will send to you."

I also put in there, "I love your sexy body/love your dirty mind, I love it when you hold me and grab me from behind..." (from the Traveling Wilbury's).

Bob wrote back, "I have no idea where you got my e-mail address, but I will gladly pay the person who provided it. You made my day!!!"

The next day I told him a joke about the Polock, the Italian and the Mexican steel workers. And the next day the one about the O'Leary twins getting drunk at the bar.

Bob sent me jokes, the ones that went around when Mike Tyson bit off Evander Holyfield's ear.

Every morning something new turned up in our e-mails.

I told Bob to believe in miracles.

Bob told me his doctor advised him to drop a few pounds, go out dancing, smoke an occasional cigar and before the end of the year, he'd be able to part his hair again.

For seven months, every morning, unless I didn't have computer access, I wrote Bobby a note. I started each e-mail with "Dear Roberto" and closed with "Love, Burtoni".

Bob went through five months of chemo and two months of radiation. Even for Ranger Bob it was almost too much. He was weak. He was scared. He was nauseated. He lost his hair, and was in pain most of the time. He couldn't sleep, but then he hadn't slept through the night since returning from Viet Nam.

He never missed a day of work.

My wife, Wendy and I visited Bob, and his wife Irma, in San Diego. His law firm had season tickets for the Padres, San Diego's major league baseball team. The seats were on the first base line, close to the action. We went to two games that summer and the first thing we did when we got to the stadium was get our provisions. Four drafts of Bud, a few bags of peanuts and four juicy Polish dogs loaded with spicy mustard and kraut. Heaven on Earth.

On our second visit the pre-game ceremony was dedicated to cancer survivors. A local oncologist threw out the first pitch. Scores of survivors of all ages stood on the foul lines as the fans cheered their victories.

At the end of the game, players from both teams gathered in the infield to pray. Brett Butler, an infielder for the Dodgers, had just returned to the lineup after a yearlong bout with throat cancer. He told the crowd he was blessed to be alive and playing the game he loved. Bob, Irma, Wendy and I stood in the stands holding each other and thanking God for this baseball blessing.

I invited Bob and Irma to our annual Passover Seder that spring, but the chemo was just starting and he had to stay close to home. The Passover Seder is the springtime gathering celebrating the Jews' escape from slavery in Egypt. God spoke to Moses from the burning bush and said, "Go tell Pharaoh to free the Jews." Moses argued with God, "I am not the man for the job." God leaned on him. Moses gave in. He went down to Egypt and told Pharaoh what God had instructed him to say. Pharaoh wasn't impressed. But after ten plagues, Pharaoh finally relented and said to Moses, "GO, NOW! GET OUT OF HERE!" The Jews headed north to the Promised Land.

It is a story of courage and persistence, escape and survival.

Bob promised he would celebrate the Seder with us the following year.

Bob and Irma were at the next Seder, and no one has ever been happier to be at the Passover table than Robert S. Brewer. He was in the Promised Land, surrounded by love, eating traditional Jewish foods and singing songs of freedom.

I am sure that out there in the desert, God must have said to Moses, "I am with you Moses, every step of the way."

When I said those words to Bobby, I didn't know how things were going to work out. I just knew we were in this together.

When I call Bob now, I tell his secretary it's Bob Dylan. Bob gets on the line and says, "So Mr. Dylan, have you taken those voice lessons yet?"

He sent me this card last week:

*Burtoni,*
*I recently passed the five year mark on post-treatment time for lymphoma. I could not have reached this point without your support, prayers and e-mails. You are a great friend and I appreciate you more than I can express.*
*I love you,*
*Roberto*

L'CHAIM...TO LIFE!

## SNYDER'S HONEY MUSTARD PRETZELS AND GOD

I had been angry at Scott for over a year, but I never said a word to him. We had been inseparable friends for two decades, but something had gone very wrong.

The relationship had always been an attraction of opposites. I am a stocky, five-foot-six, one hundred and eighty pound meso-morph. Scott is a sinewy five-foot-ten, one hundred and twenty pound ectomorph. I am a successful corporate motivational trainer. Scott, over the past 25 years, has had at least ten jobs, going for months at a time without employment, often having to borrow money from friends and family to buy gasoline for his truck and canned chili for dinner.

At the time of our drift, I had been married for five years in my second marriage. My first marriage had lasted twenty-two years. I was an active father to my three children. Scott had been married to his pregnant wife for six months when he realized that it was not going to work out. He left but made sure he saw his son, Peter, at least once or twice a year and stayed in touch by telephone calls and letters.

I spent much of my youth playing tennis and golf with my father at upper middle-class country clubs. Scott's early years were spent exploring the southwestern deserts in an old Jeep with his dad.

When Scott returned from his tour of duty in Viet Nam, he became the most accomplished rock climber in Arizona. I got shaky legs and vertigo if I was fifteen feet off the ground.

I live in a four bedroom, two bathroom house, with two cars, a TV, a front and back lawn. For years, Scott chose a hermit existence, in a trailer on the prairie, with an outhouse, no running water, tele-phone or electricity. An ice chest kept his Budweiser a few degrees cooler than room temperature. A wood stove heated the water that he poured over himself in his make-shift shower stall.

I consulted with some of America's largest corporations. Scott disdained all things corporate. He looked derisively upon company drones, and raged against the "Big Business" rape of Mother Earth.

Scott was by any estimation, especially his father's and my mother's, financially unsuccessful. His father, a prosperous southern California businessman, had agonized over his son's self-imposed poverty. Scott's lifestyle would be difficult for most fathers to embrace, but even more so because Scott had to ask for money to carry him through the rough times.

His father found this pattern a constant source of irritation, embarrassment and worry. But still his love for his son outweighed all his disappointments.

My mother's feelings about Scott were more complex. Although she never said that she wanted me to end my friendship with Scott, she would frequently hint that Scott was partially responsible for eroding my already limited resolve to achieve financial greatness. She was also not thrilled that Scott had introduced me to rock climbing, an activity she considered to be irresponsible at best. Scott's lifestyle--and my attraction to it--jangled every cell in her maternal body. He became the target of her verbal barbs whenever the three of us got together. Scott was always a good sport about it.

Despite his dogged determination to avoid anything resembling traditional American success, Scott was and still is a legend, respected throughout the entire country as a rock climbing pioneer. But more importantly, Scott is dearly loved by all who have been blessed to spend any time with him.

One of the ways my mom expresses her love to my brother and me is to send us care packages of every kind of dried fruit on earth: apricots, figs, raisins, pears, peaches, prunes and cherries. She also sends us nuts from around the world: hazelnuts, peanuts, Brazil nuts, cashews, pistachios and walnuts. One year she surprised us with Honey Mustard Pretzels made by Snyder's of Hanover, an old Pennsylvania pretzel company. What a treat! Spiced with tangy mustard, just enough honey and baked into a crisp pretzel. Mom knows food! And Mom knows her boys.

Scott was at my house the first time Mom sent the pretzels. We opened the box. We munched, we drooled, we smiled. We praised Mom and we washed the pretzels down with a few of our favorite imported beers. Snyder's Honey Mustard Pretzels! Scott and I had a new ritual.

Snyder's Pretzels were there for me on my next visit to Mom's Laguna Hills house. When it was time to head back to Arizona, we began the long goodbyes. Mom surprised me with two boxes of Snyder's Honey Mustard Pretzels, and the explicit instructions: "Don't give either of these to Scott."

Stunned, but without a moment's hesitation, I handed back both boxes. She was startled, but she got the message. Mom handed the boxes back to me and retracted her No Scott Rule.

In retrospect, I know the pretzel embargo was ill conceived and never had a chance of working. In one response, I blocked the pretzel embargo, maintained the delicate balance of power between Mom and me, and protected the honor of my friend, Scott Baxter.

If it was only this simple, the headlines in the morning paper might have read: Middle-aged Man Stands Up For Friend's Honor. But it wasn't that simple. My career as a corporate team builder was beginning to grow, and I was working for some of the largest corporations in the country. I sometimes wore silk ties, dry-cleaned wool slacks and fancy sports jackets. My hair was trimmed and I shaved nearly every morning.

None of this sat well with Scott. He was also spending a lot of his time with two of our community's most impassioned social activists--and I had slipped over the line into enemy territory.

Big Business was good for me and my family. And I was even starting to like the people I worked with. Most of them were hard-working, honest, family-oriented folks who woke up every morning and tried to do the best for their families, employees and customers. There was hardly a stereotypical company clone amongst them.

When Scott and I got together for breakfast or a weekend adventure, I no longer spoke about my work. I feared Scott's caustic judgments. They came anyway. Few were frontal assaults, but I was stung by an unrelenting barrage of veiled ambushes. I began to dislike the time I spent with Scott.

I fantasized every day about telling him off. Calling him on his self-righteous, hypocritical crap. But I never had the guts to say anything. I stewed in my bitterness and plotted scathing but unlaunched counterattacks. My heart ached every day for our old friendship.

Scott's disdain felt like a twisted dagger between my ribs. It was excruciatingly painful to go through the motions of my life and my most valued friendship--as if everything was just fine.

The date for our next desert outing was set. We would climb Big Horn Peak, a rugged mountain in an isolated area eighty miles west of Phoenix. The first order of business was to pick up our fellow adventurer, Avtar, who was flying into Phoenix's Sky Harbor Airport from San Francisco, where he served in an Army intelligence unit. Avtar rarely missed our desert outings, even when he had been stationed in Georgia for three years. We knew that army life was exacting a huge toll from him and our adventures to the desert were no less than life-sustaining for him.

I drove through a parking lot on our way to the airport. Scott chastised me for driving over a set of speed bumps, and not around them. It was a bad start.

At the terminal, I wandered into the duty free store, ignoring the sign stating that only international passengers were allowed. After poking around for a minutes, I came out.

Scott pointed at the sign and looked at me like I was an idiot. "Can't you read?" he said. It was the last straw. No more. "Oh, and of course you abide by all of the rules?" I said.

I vowed to myself the sun would not go down without my putting an end, one way or another, to this bullshit.

We greeted Avtar as if everything was fine, drove back to our rendezvous point, where Avtar loaded himself and his gear into our friend Sevak's' pickup, and we were off to the desert.

Scott and I were alone in my red Jeep Grand Cherokee. I was at the wheel. He had no idea what was coming, and neither did I. All I knew for sure was that my silence was about to be broken. I shook with pent-up anger. We hadn't pulled away from Sevak's house before I ripped into Scott. "What the fuck has been going on? You treat me like I am your fuckin' worst enemy."

We drove south on 7th Street, then headed west on I-10. Between the two of us we had traveled this stretch of highway at least a hundred times over the past thirty years, either on our adventures to the desert or on our way to the coast to visit family. I was on cruise control--and I was on a roll. Scott had no choice but to listen. He was belted in, the doors were locked and we were cruisin' down the freeway.

At first he looked puzzled. "Give me some examples," he said. I obliged.

I gave him examples--a lot of them. I reeled them off, one after another. Taken separately, each incident could have been explained away, but the stack of evidence was unequivocal. I was way past caring about anything but ridding myself of the bile that had built up inside me. It was my turn now. Time stopped as we sped past the billboards of west Phoenix. I watched them fade away in my rear view mirror. Somewhere, miles past the last housing development and strip mall, I began to feel some relief. The pretending was over. Scott listened and heard every word. When I finally said everything I needed to say and was able to take a breath, there was silence.

With pained sadness, Scott agreed. And while initially stunned by my attack, he was relieved. We had loved each other too deeply, for too long, for this ugliness to continue.

He told me he had also been taking his aggression out on his sister Marion, the other dearest person in his life. Marion was a successful psychologist in northern California, living a comfortable middle-class lifestyle.

Scott spoke with an honesty and regret that began to soften my hardened heart. He said that he had hoped the people he loved the most would be able to tolerate his verbal attacks, but he knew his intolerance had grown out of control. His enemies had become anyone who was living above his minimalist standards. His primary targets were me and Marion. He didn't want to hurt us. Not really. He was hurting. He had backed himself into a corner--and was bitter towards anyone who was not consumed with the same bitterness.

Scott knew he was going to have to make some big decisions in his life, and soon. We were both crying now. We had missed each other deeply and it was time to put this awful year behind us.

We were done talking. Suddenly in the distance, there was a huge industrial building off to the south that neither of us had ever seen before. We both read the huge sign the same time. It read Snyder's of Hanover. We turned to each other, stunned, tears still streaming down our cheeks. It was over. The war was over.

If you are ever driving west of Phoenix on I-10 , look off to the south when you get about thirty miles from town. See if there is a Snyder's pretzel factory just off the road. If it is there, slow down and give it an appreciative nod. If it is not, well, that's okay, too.

## BORN AGAIN FRIENDS

Some of my best friends are born again Christians. I am Jewish. These friends are not lockstep in their opinions, but they are basically against abortion, assisted suicide or euthanasia, in favor of prayer in public schools, opposed to gay marriage, and in favor of teaching creationism and intelligent design in our science classes.

I line up on a different side of a lot of those issues--and some of the highest profile spokesmen for America's Religious Right scare the hell out of me. Two days after 9/11, Jerry Falwell said, "Abortionists have got to bear some burden for this because God will not be mocked." Pat Robertson was quoted on his 700 Club television program, "You say you're supposed to be nice to the Episcopalians and the Presbyterians and the Methodists and this and that and the other thing. NONSENSE! I don't have to be nice to the spirit of the Antichrist."

YOW!

Matt Evans, Matt Repucci and Ron Mann are dear to me. Each of them has chosen Jesus as his personal savior.

Matt Evans was a banker when we first met. I didn't like him from the start. Matt was assigned to oversee the takeover of my beloved small town Pima Savings and Loan. It was ugly. I sneered at him everytime I made a deposit as he sat behind the teller line but I tried not to make it too obvious.

Once the takeover was finalized, Matt became the manager at what became my new bank. I saw him at least two times every week when I made my deposits. He was nice to me. I was nice to him. I got over it. After all, the takeover was just a business deal.

I'm basically a chatty guy. So is Matt. I love to laugh. Matt loves to laugh. It didn't take long before I looked forward to seeing him. It appeared Matt looked forward to seeing me too.

Later that month, I presented a program for parents at DeMiguel Elementary School where his daughters attended. I called it, "The Rock 'n' Roll of Family Relationships." It was divided into three weekly segments: Yakkity Yak (don't talk back), R-E-S-P-E-C-T and Love Me Tender. Matt and his wife Jennifer were in the audience, and they loved it.

The following week, Matt introduced me to his boss, Paulie Olson. "You have to hire Burt to work with our management team," Matt said. Paulie hired me. He hired me at least ten more times after that.

Matt and I started to hang out. Good food. Good talk. At first we talked business, but as time went on we talked less business and just enjoyed each other. Mostly we laughed. We got serious too. Every lunch started with a prayer. Two men, with their heads bowed. Matt's prayer ended with, "In Jesus' name, we pray." My prayer ended with, "Thank you, God, for our blessings."

We talked about everything. One day Matt came clean, "I got to tell you, I didn't like how you sneered at me when we first met during the takeover."

I told him, "I got caught up in the staff's anger over the little bank being taken over by the BIG BANK. I'm usually on the side of the little guy. I'm sorry."

Matt and I agree on sushi, and we really agree on Hiro's, our favorite sushi restaurant. I pick Matt up for lunch and pop in music from Bob Dylan's Christian years: *Property of Jesus*, *Shot of Love*, *When He Returns* and *Gotta Serve Somebody*. Matt and I sing along with our best nasal Dylan imitations.

I have always loved Bob Dylan. Matt loves Jesus. Matt and I love each other. Matt finally loves Bob Dylan. And I appreciate Jesus more than I ever thought I would.

Every two weeks, we weave through traffic on our way to the sushi bar, a Jew and a born again Christian wailing in full blown rapture.

In 1972 Ron Mann was a skinny kid running cross-country for Northern Arizona University. I was in graduate school, and I followed the team--which was loaded with national class runners. Ron wasn't one of them. He was solid, but not exceptional.

Eight years later, after coaching high school track and field in Phoenix, Ron returned to NAU to be head coach of the men's and women's cross-country and track and field teams. During his ensuing twenty plus years at NAU he became one of the most successful coaches in the country. He won fifty-eight conference championships and fifty-seven Coach of the Year awards. He coached one hundred and seven All-Americans and five Olympians. He became a legend.

When phenom sophomore distance runner and devout Muslim, Nurani Sheik, was struggling with a potential career-ending anxiety disorder, Ron told him, "Nurani, it's okay with me if you never run again. I just want to see you happy."

Ron, Nurani, and I sat in Ron's office and prayed for God's guidance. Nurani decided take some time off from his studies and return home to his family in Salt Lake City. A year later, Ron was offered the head coaching position at University of Louisville. Nurani and his family followed. He staged a brilliant comeback earning the number one spot on the Louisville cross-country team.

Nurani still looks to Ron, his coach and father figure, for advice and support. Nurani hasn't seen his own father in fifteen years, after soldiers in Somalia burned his house and drove his family away.

Before Ron left to coach at Louisville, we met every two to three weeks for lunch at Oregano's Italian Restaurant. We always split the Oregano's Favorite salad with chicken and we began every meal with a prayer. Ron ended his prayer, "In Jesus' name, we pray." I ended my prayer with "Thank you God for our blessings."

I have never met Matt Repucci in person. He works for Mac-Connection, a huge computer catalogue company in New Hampshire. I called their 800 number one day looking for some computer advice.

"Hello, this is Matt, how can I help you today?"

I think I cracked a joke. He laughed. That's how it started. Since then we've talked on the telephone and exchanged e-mail messages more than a hundred times.

Now, I send him my short stories. He sends me pictures of his family. We talk every few weeks. When I call him, he picks up his line and says, "Hello, this is Matt, how can I help you today?"

After a theatrically long pause, I respond, "Matt REPUCCI?"

"Gershater!" Matt laughs, "How are you doing?"

And we are off. We've been doing this for two years, maybe three. I buy a computer or a camera once in a while, but that's not what keeps us connected. We talk hiking. We talk family. Somewhere along the line I told him about our huge Passover Seder. He told me about his Bible study.

He's going to bring his family to Arizona next year. I told him they can stay with us. We'll hike. We'll talk. Matt Repucci and I will have lunch together. And it is my best guess, that before we eat our first bite, we will bow our heads, and the Jew and the Christian will each thank God for our blessings.

# COMMITMENT IS NOT A FEELING

We commit to our spouses--for better or for worse. We commit to our children--for better or for worse. My dear friend Christy commited to her very difficult, alcohol and drug addicted, near homeless brother Dan--for better or for worse.

It is easy to keep a commitment when it is 'for better'. It is the 'for worse' part that makes commitment hard. If commitment was only 'for better', we wouldn't need a special word for it. We would just do what feels good, and there are already a few words designated for that.

Commitment doesn't always feel good while you're doing it, but in the wise words of one of my dear clients, "You sleep better."

Why is sleeping better so important?

Because when it's dark outside we can't fool ourselves as easily.

## MOVING MOM I

"Five dollars for those five records? That's an insult. They're worth a lot more than that!" Mom said to the gentleman rummaging through her forty-year-old record collection.

"I think it's a fair offer," he replied. He held *My Fair Lady, West Side Story*, a nondescript Frank Sinatra, and two classical albums, all of them scratched.

"Thank you very much ma'am. Good luck with your move." He returned the albums to their pile and ambled out the door towards his 1982 Dodge beater.

Mom was a bit surprised he did not make a higher offer.

On the way to his car he peeked into the dumpster I was filling with old books, dated travel guides and road maps, broken chairs, half filled bottles of booze, melted candles, chipped porcelain coffee cups, decade old cans of green beans and tuna and a massive collection of wood screws.

Mom wouldn't need these things in the assisted living facility.

She was eighty-two, ravaged by rheumatoid arthritis, on daily meds, yet nearly always in pain.

The old collector looked more deeply into the dumpster. His eyes lit up. "Those are some fine books." he said. "And those travel guides." Ever the gentleman, he walked back and called politely through the screen door, "Ma'am, there are a few things in the dumpster I'm interested in. Would it be all right if I took them?"

"No," Mom answered. "I have plans for those."

The man turned around and headed back to his car, seemingly unfazed. I was not unfazed. I vaulted into the dumpster and said, "Excuse me sir, tell me what you want."

"Are you sure?" he looked nervously back at the screen door.

I assured him it was fine.

We filled the back seat of the Dodge with dumpster goodies. He thanked me. We shook hands and he drove away.

I stood alone in the yard. It was quiet. I thought about what had brought my mom and me to this day.

Three weeks earlier, Jim, my mom's boyfriend and caretaker, had left. Anger and confusion had driven him off. He was dedicated to my mother--and he suffered from Alzheimer's disease. He became increasingly disoriented and agitated.

They had hired a cook. The breaking point came one evening as Jim and the new cook were in the kitchen. My mom sat at the dining room table. She became increasingly angered by Jim's puttering around the kitchen. Finally she blew.

"I really let him have it," she later admitted to me.

I knew it was bad. Mom had never acknowledged any of her venomous tongue lashings to me.

After the kitchen scene, they went to bed that night as usual. When Jim awoke the next morning, he remembered the incident from the night before and dialed 9-1-1! He convinced the dispatcher he was in immediate danger. He woke Mom and told her the ambulance was coming to take her away.

A few minutes later, the sheriff, a community security guard, and an ambulance arrived. The sheriff questioned Jim and Mom, trying to piece together the events of the previous evening. Mom was verbally astute and convincing. Jim's Alzheimer's had robbed him of words. He couldn't plead his case. The sheriff listened, evaluated and then warned Jim, "Don't be making anymore trouble around here or we'll have to take you in." With a "Have a nice day," he left them to sort out their lives.

After the sheriff left, Jim called an attorney and convinced him he was being abused by Mom. Within two days the lawyer moved Jim into an assisted living home a few miles from Mom and took charge of his finances. He also facilitated the removal of Jim's possessions from Mom's house, including Jim's side of the adjoined twin beds.

The next morning, sleeping alone for the first time in nine years, Mom rolled over to answer the telephone. The night stand hadn't been replaced by the movers. She rolled off the bed and toppled to the floor, fracturing her right wrist and shoulder. Somehow she was able to call 9-1-1. The ambulance took her to the emergency room where the doctors put a cast on her wrist and a sling on her arm. Now, she was now completely incapacitated.

Mom had to arrange for twenty-four hour care before she was alllowed to return home. Mom didn't know about care-givers or how to find one. God must have intervened; Manny, a Philippino guardian angel somehow showed up and offered his care-giving services to Mom. He was a gentle, energetic man with a delightful laugh. He dressed Mom, bathed her, cooked three meals a day, did the shopping, cleaned the house and catered to her every desire. Mom soldiered on, although she missed Jim terribly--and was in excruciating pain. She faced her new reality, hired a realtor, and within a month she sold her house.

During that time, Mom and Jim talked every day. Jim complained about his new assisted living home and his gouging lawyer. "Please let me come home," he begged. "I won't cause any trouble, please, Regina." He was lonely and scared.

Mom cried everyday, knowing Jim did too. Their frequent phone calls brought them comfort--and fueled their loneliness. They wanted to turn back time and hold each other every night in bed. But their failing capacities made a reunion seem remote.

After Mom sold the house she made plans to move to an assisted living facilty in Camarillo, my brother Howie's home town, two hours north. Would she and Jim ever see each other again? Mom and I made arrangements with Jim to eat lunch at his facility a few days before the move north. When we arrived, Jim had already eaten. He forgot our lunch date.

With the moving van packed, we headed to her new home at the Villa La Paloma Assisted Care Facility. The two hour ride was subdued. As we entered the lobby of Mom's new home, we were greeted by the black felt announcement board:

BINGO TONIGHT
WELCOME REGINA GERSHATER

We found her room and began to unload the truck. It felt like we were building a stage set. In only a few hours, paintings, photographs, statues, dressers, file cabinets, bedding, couches, the microwave, a small table, plants, clocks, throw rugs, towels, TV's were in place. It was a mini-replica of her home in Laguna Hills. We took pictures, reminders of this day that we wished wasn't happening.

After dinner, my daughter Jessie and I kissed Mom goodnight. We left her in the hands of a friendly Nigerian aide. Mom thanked us. We told her we'd see her in the morning. We held back our tears until we were in the parking lot.

Mom settled in. She and I talked regularly. I was relieved by what I heard--and proud. Mom was making the best of it. The food was OK. The care, for the most part, was acceptable. She enjoyed the daily activities.

She was making friends, although not with the administrators. She was already an outspoken member on a committee to improve resident services. This was her new life and she was dealing with it.

Jim, on the other hand, was terrified of living out his last days alone. He called her everyday, "Please, Regina, please." Mom cried but she couldn't do anything.

Jim's lawyer had made himself Jim's legal guardian. Mom was blocked. But Mom is at her best when she's blocked. She called Jim's lawyer. Asked him hard questions about the money he was getting for his services. Accused him of taking advantage of Jim's mental state.

Threatened him with bar complaints and lawsuits. Said she'd write a letter to the Leisure World News, exposing him to the community. He would be sorry.

She didn't let up. She called day after day. It didn't take more than a week before the poor guy caved in. He wrote a letter to the court excusing himself from all legal and fiduciary responsibilities. He was done.

Mom contacted a doctor to evaluate Jim's mental condition. She became Jim's legal guardian. She had his money transferred to her account. She hired a moving van, and in a little over a week, Jim took a taxi to Camarillo and moved into his one bedroom apartment upstairs from Mom.

Now, Mom and Jim eat their meals together. They watch TV every night side by side. They go on field trips to local historical sites. Jim pushes her wheel chair and Mom gives him directions. They are inseparable, except at night when they go to to bed. Mom prefers it this way.

Jim's memory is fading. Mom's arthritis is unrelenting--but now they no longer ache to be with each other.

## MOVING MOM II

A year passed in my mom's life at Villa La Paloma Assisted Living Facility--mostly without event.

Mom had gotten to know and enjoy most of the residents, though she thought they were too docile--unwilling or unable to speak up for their rights. Mom became their self-appointed spokesperson. She fought the good fight at every turn, unable or unwilling to let any perceived injustice or service flaw go unmentioned.

She did her best to improve food service, evening movie choices, daily van schedule, and the general attitude of the administrative staff. In return, she received a letter from the director warning her she would have to leave the facility if there were more complaints.

Jim's Alzheimer's worsened. His short-term memory slipped every week. Loquacious prior to his disease, he struggled in conversation. Frustrated, he withdrew.

And he fidgeted incessantly, sorting though his wallet and keys. "Is this key to my car?" He hadn't driven his car for over a year.

His whistling habit increased. Mom admonished him, "Jim, put those things away. Stop whistling. You're driving me crazy!"

He became progressively disoriented. Mom covered for him. She got him to meals on time. Made sure his bills were paid. Gave him his medicine. After dinner they watched TV together. She prepared him for bed, kissed him goodnight and struggled back to her room, leaning heavily on her walker. The next morning she returned to help him pick out clothes and take him to breakfast.

My brother Howie and my sister-in-law Lihi live two miles up the street from Villa La Paloma. When Mom first moved in, they were trying to survive in the wake of the death of their son, David. He had been thrown from a friend's Suburban the summer before.

Mom moved to be close to family. Bad timing. Worse chemistry. Howie visited Mom and Jim every week or so, depending upon who you asked. Lihi went less frequently. The two children, Tammy and Brian were too involved with their own lives to visit often.

But Mom is a survivor. She didn't sit around. She and Jim took every field trip offered by the Villa. They went to museums, to malls, to state parks. They attended every lecture and most evening movies. And Mom never missed a Villa La Paloma community meeting, where she could air her "suggestions" to the administration.

That first year, I visited three times from Arizona, for short stays, two to three days. We talked, we went shopping and we ate at local restaurants. My three children visited from Oregon, Idaho and Arizona during the year.

Mom wasn't ecstatic about the arrangement, but she made the best of it. I suspect the Villa director felt the same way. Howie was her main social outlet and I didn't have to think about it very much...ten hours away in Arizona.

Jim's condition worsened. Mom scheduled an appointment with his doctor, hoping something could slow his mental deterioration. The doctor said nothing could be done. Alzheimer's Disease is progressive and incurable. A diagnosis was sent to the Villa: Alzheimer's disease, mid-to-late stage. A week later, Mom received a letter from the director of Villa La Paloma that read something like this:

*Dear Regina,*                                                    *April 3, 2005*
*We have recently received a medical report for Jim Conly from Dr. Allan Stuart. Jim has been diagnosed with Alzheimer's disease. Villa La Paloma is not licensed by the State of California to care for residents who are in the latter stages of Alzheimer's disease.*
*As you have Power of Attorney in matters regarding Jim Conly, please be advised that we are no longer able to continue providing services to him at our facility. We are giving you thirty days from this notification to make different living arrangements for Mr. Conly.*
*Thank you for your cooperation in this matter.*
*Sincerely,*
*Marla Mason*
*Director, Villa La Paloma*

Mom was shocked--and angry. She called Howie. "Howard, we have to look for a new place. They say they can't keep Jim here anymore."

For a few weeks, Howie and Mom explored other facilities. None of them worked--for Mom. They were either too old or too expensive. One didn't have enough closet space. Another was too far from Howie's house.

As the search grew more and more futile, my oldest daughter, Jennie, began calling Mom from Arizona. "Grandma," she would say, "what about Sedona? You've been there. It's only forty-five minutes from our house and you will love it. Come live there. And there are a lot of people who will visit. Follow your heart, Grandma."

Mom called me. "I think I want to live in Sedona," she said.
Mom called me again. "I am moving to Sedona."
She hadn't told Howie yet.

Jennie and I took a quick trip to California to make plans.

Howie was furious. "She'll freeze in those mountains. I've been there. She is not going to Sedona, period!"

"If it's too cold." Mom said. "I'll move back."

## MOVING MOM III

I had no idea that moving Mom to Arizona would have so much impact on everyone, especially my brother Howie and me. The tension between us was more than unsettling. Howard was upset. Still, he invited me to go to a Dodger-Giants game. "Hell no," I thought. I shook my head. "I came here to spend time with Mom," I said.

Later, Jennie gave me some daughterly advice. "Dad, you should go with Howie. Lihi thinks so too." I still didn't want to go but Jennie was right. This was an opportunity. My brother and I couldn't heal this rift over moving Mom unless we spent time together.

A little after noon, Howie, Brian, two of Brian's friends, and I piled in to Howie's 1985 Lincoln Town Car. Howie and I were in the front. The young guys were in the back. "Hey Howie," I heard from the back seat, "I got laid last night."

"That's great, Robby." Howie laughed. "How was it?"

"It was fantastic, Howie."

We drove the LA freeways to Dodger Stadium. Tension from the morning conflict about Mom hung heavy. The CD player blasted rap music. Sex. Violence. Expletive. BOOM BA BA BOOM. BOOM BA BA BOOM. Sex. Violence. Expletive. BOOM BA BA BOOM. BOOM BA BOOM.

"What the hell did I get myself into?" I thought.

BOOM BA BA BOOM. BOOM BA BA BOOM. FUCK THIS. SUCK THAT.

I was losing it fast. Ready to scream. "Don't blow it Burt," I thought to myself.

The words of Carolyn Myss, a wonderful spiritual teacher, came to me. "It's easy to hold your center in a garden, sitting cross-legged next to a bubbling fountain. ANYONE CAN DO THAT!" Carolyn snaps. "The real challenge is to keep your serenity when you are in chaos."

I took a few deep breaths. I remembered my dear friend Saint Albert's advice. He has it programed on his computer screen saver: PYAO (Pray Your Ass Off).

I prayed my ass off. I called in every spiritual lesson I ever learned: I took slow full breaths. I returned to my senses and got out of my head. I visualized Divine light streaming down through my body.

The music blared on. It stopped bothering me. The awkwardness of not talking stopped bothering me.

"Thank you, God."

"Thank you, Carolyn."

"Thank you, Saint Albert."

"Thank you everyone who ever gave me spiritual guidance."

I was calm. I was thankful to be alive and going to a Dodger-Giant game with my brother.

I looked over at Howie. His jaw was set. "What the fuck are you thinking, taking Mom to Sedona," Howie said. "It's freezing there!"

"I've lived in Northern Arizona thirty-five years. It's not that freakin' cold."

"I've been there Burt! Her body can't take it."

"She'll stay inside when it's cold," I said.

"For four months?"

"Howard, this is not Vermont, it's Arizona."

"Besides," he said, "you and Jennie have been sneaking around my back. I've been working for a month trying to find a place for her. You undermined me."

The boys in the back seat were silent.

The battle went on. We hit the Dodger Stadium traffic, still fuming. We parked and got out of the car, still fuming. The boys went ahead--glad to leave us behind.

Howie and I headed to the stadium. Side by side. Without looking at me, Howie said, "Let's enjoy the game."

I was still in battle mode. I remembered Carolyn Myss. "We are more terrified of change than we are of death!"

Bingo. I could make peace if I took off my armor, holstered my guns. I could do it right now. If I wanted to.

"You're right Howie, let's enjoy the game."

We hugged. We cried. Hundreds of fans streamed by us.

I told Howie I hadn't kept him in the loop about moving Mom to Arizona.

"I'm sorry," I said.

"Thanks, brother."

We needed one more ticket for the game. We began looking for the ticket office.

We couldn't find one. Howie spotted an LA cop. "Do you know where we can we get a ticket?" Howie asked.

The officer looked at us for a second, "Hold on, let me talk to my partner."

"You got those extra tickets?" His pal studied us briefly. He took a ticket from his pocket and handed it to Howie. "Enjoy the game."

"How much is it?" Howie reached for his wallet.

The officer grinned, "No charge."

Howie and I looked at each other, thanked both officers and headed to our seats.

Howie and I sat a few seats behind the boys. The game was boring until the last inning. The Dodgers were behind 4-3. Jason Phillips at the plate for the Dodgers. Two outs, bases loaded. The count was three balls and no strikes. Phillips got his pitch and sliced a single just past the second baseman into right center, driving in the winning run. Dodger Stadium erupted.

We walked back to the parking lot, the boys seemed uneasy. Howie and I waited until we were all in the Lincoln to tell them the fight was over. The boys applauded us from the back seat.

Two weeks later, Wendy and I drove to Los Angeles to bring Mom and Jim to Arizona. The family gathered at Villa La Paloma for a going-away supper.

There were eight of us, Howie, Lihi and the kids, Wendy and me, Mom and Jim. The food was simple, the atmosphere complex. Lihi showed her photos from her and Brian's recent trip to Israel and Egypt. Mom thanked all of us for being with her and Jim. Howie wished us all good luck on the journey to Arizona.

It was my turn. I pulled a package from under my chair and stood next to Howie. He looked up at me. I don't remember my exact words, but I remember they were filled with my love and gratitude. I presented my brother with a street sign that read EBBETS FIELD AVENUE. (The Dodgers had played at Ebbets Field in Brooklyn before they moved to Los Angeles in 1959.)

Howie held it to his heart. "Thanks, brother.

## MOVING MOM IV

After our farewell dinner Mom and Jim went back to their room. Jim was frantic. He paced. He fretted. He tested and retested the key in their door lock. He opened and closed the windows. He could not be still. "Please, Regina," he said, "Give me a pill."

Wendy and I stayed as long as we could and then went back to our room. We told Mom we would be ready to roll at 5:00 AM to get an early start.

We showed up at their room the next morning. Five o'clock. Jim was moving slower than usual. Mom had given him one of her pills so he could get to sleep. We loaded them and their suitcases into our car. We bade farewell to Villa La Paloma and headed east toward the Mojave desert.

Before Alzheimer's, Jim was a real talker. Jim didn't talk for the first three hours of the trip. He slept. We woke him for breakfast at IHOP. I walked him to the restroom. His eyes were glazed. He stood at the urinal for nearly ten minutes with the task in hand. I watched. I waited. I watched. Finally, he released. Breakfast was no faster. Over an hour later, we got back into the car and continued the journey. Jim went back to sleep.

Later that evening we arrived at their new home, Sedona Winds Assisted Living Facility. Wendy and I helped them settle in. We kissed them good night, gave the front desk supervisor our number just in case and headed home to Flagstaff, fifty minutes away. It was 9:00 PM. We were tired and ready to sleep. It was a long day.

Less than twenty miles up the road, my cell phone rang. It was Sedona Winds.

"Your mother and Jim got into a fight. Please come back down to help sort this thing out."

I sighed, "We'll be right there."

Wendy rolled her eyes.

"We gotta go back," I said. She grinned.

"Honey, I know this is weird," I said, "but this is perfect."

"I was thinking the same thing," Wendy said. "We need a plan."

By the time we pulled into the parking lot we had The Plan: Jim needed to be taken to the nearest hospital emergency department and evaluated. Reality had struck--sooner than we had guessed.

We walked into Sedona Winds. Jim was speaking to the desk clerk. He was agitated. Wendy skillfully diverted him to a chair across the lobby.

I turned to the desk clerk, "What happened?"

"Jim hit your mom."

"What!?"

"That's what your mom told us."

"I need to talk to my mom." I nodded to Wendy and headed down the hall to the guest apartment.

Mom sat at the dining room table. She looked up in surprise. "Why are you here?"

"They called me. What happened"?

She started to cry. "Jim wouldn't stay in the room. I tried to stop him. I shouldn't have. He hit me."

"Here's what we gotta do, Mom. We have to get Jim evaluated pronto--tonight. I'll be right back."

I went back to the front desk. The desk clerk looked up.

"Here's what needs to be done," I said.

Before I could go on, the desk clerk said, "I've already spoken to the director. She offered two options.

"One, you or Wendy stay here with your mom and Jim. Two, you take Jim back to Flagstaff for the night."

He had to be kidding. "Here's what I think," I said. "Call an ambulance and let's get Jim to the Verde Valley Medical Center for an evaluation right away."

Ten minutes later the Sedona Fire Department showed up. I told them The Plan.

"Do you have Power Of Attorney?" the paramedic asked.

"No, my mom does."

"I need to to talk with her," he said.

I led him to the room.

"Hi, Mrs. Gershater. How are you doing."

"OK." Mom smiled, but she had tears in her eyes.

"Your son and I have discussed the situation. I think it would best for Jim to be evaluated immediately."

"Does he have to go somewhere?"

"Not very far. Verde Valley Medical Center is half an hour away. Their emergency room is set up to handle this kind of situation."

My mom shook her head, "I don't want him to go. I can't drive. I won't be able to see him there."

"Mom," I said, "This is our only option. I'll take you there tomorrow."

"Mrs. Gershater," the paramedic said gently, "Sedona Winds isn't set up for Jim's level of confusion. They won't let him stay here."

Mom was quiet, and then she put her head down and sobbed.

The paramedic and I waited.

Finally she raised her head, "If that's what we have to do, that's what we have to do."

They put Jim in the ambulance and drove him to the hospital. Wendy rode with Jim. I followed. Jim had mellowed out by the time he was admitted to the emergency room.

Three hours later, after extensive interviews with the doctor and social worker, a decision was made. Jim would be placed in their Senior Behavioral Health Unit for observation and evaluation. Wendy and I were relieved. We kissed him goodnight, gave Mom a quick call with the update and drove home. We finally climbed into bed somewhere around 2:00 AM.

Jim stayed in the hospital for three more weeks. The doctors, psychologists, social workers and nurses determined he could no longer stay in a standard assisted living facility. He was frequently disoriented, and he was a flight risk. He needed an Alzheimer's unit with close supervision and locks on the doors.

The social worker called Mom. "Regina, Jim can't be in assisted living anymore. His condition won't allow it. Unfortunately, there are no rooms available near you. The closest one is in Prescott, an hour away."

"I won't consent to that!" Mom said. "It's too far away. I won't be able to see him. I won't agree to sending him to Prescott."

"I'm sorry, Regina, the only available bed is in Prescott. He can't stay here any longer. We are an evaluation unit, not a residence facility. We've already kept him past our limit."

"It's too far away," Mom said.

The social worker called me. "Burt, could you help your mom understand that Jim needs to go to Prescott, at least until a bed is available at the Sedona Winds Alzheimer's unit?"

"I have never been very successful of convincing my mom of anything," I said. "What's your leverage if she says she won't consent? Does she have the final word?"

The social worker paused. "No, she doesn't. We can turn the case over to Adult Protective Services and claim that your mother is not making good decisions for Jim."

"If it comes that," I said, "do it."

Two days later, the social worker set up a meeting with my mom, the psychiatrist, herself and me. As Mom and I drove to the medical center, she said, "I won't give my consent."

"There aren't any other options."

We dropped the subject.

During the meeting, the social worker said, "There is room available for Jim in Prescott. They can take him today."

"No. It's too far away," Mom said softly.

"It's our only choice Mom."

She cried.

The social worker looked at me. I nodded. She picked up the phone and called the Margaret T. Morris Facility in Prescott. We drove him there the following day.

A month later, a room opened up in the dementia unit at Sedona Winds. We drove him back.

For a few weeks, Mom spent nearly every waking hour with Jim. But as Jim deteriorated, Mom became more and more tired.

Mom doesn't see Jim as much anymore. He still recognizes her and smiles when he sees her. They don't talk much. They sit and hold hands. Mom makes sure the aides give him chocolate ice cream, but she wonders how long they'll be able to keep him there.

## GOODBYE JIM

No matter how much Mom wanted to put off the inevitable, his time at Sedona Winds was drawing to a close. The nurse in charge called me. "Jim is becoming combative with the care-givers and he's exposing himself to the residents. We can't keep him here any longer."

"Aren't those behaviors normal for a person in the latter stages of Alzheimer's?" I asked.

"They are, but we are not equipped to handle residents when they reach that stage," she answered.

Mom was angry when she heard the news, but I think she was mostly scared.

"It's not his fault," she said, "every time I go to see him there's a woman trying to fondle him. It's her fault, not his. Why don't they make her leave?

"Where's he going to go?"

"I won't be able to see him."

"I'm his guardian, I won't let them."

It wasn't up to Mom anymore. And Mom knew.

The next day an ambulance took Jim to the Verde Valley Medical Center Senior Behavioral Health Unit for a second evaluation. They admitted him. A week later they asked us to attend a meeting to discuss their findings.

"Sedona Winds just wants to kick him out," she said. "I won't be able to see him, I can't drive." She began to cry. She knew we were out of options and we were running out of time.

The psychiatrist instructed us that Jim had to be placed in a behavioral unit where the staff is trained to handle disruptive patients.

"Is there a facility like that in Sedona?" Mom asked.

"No," the doctor answered. "There are only two facilities in the area."

Mom looked worried. "Where are they?"

"There is the one in Prescott. And one in Payson."

"They are both over an hour away. I won't be able to see him." Mom was pushing but she knew she didn't have any leverage.

Jim was admitted to the Rim Rock Retirement Home in Payson, Arizona. A few days later, Mom, Wendy and I drove to see him, down steep switchbacks through the rugged Mogollon Rim country. Mom loves the beauty of northern Arizona. The drive helped take her mind off our impending visit.

When we arrived, Jim was in the dining room. He smiled at Mom and puckered his lips to kiss her. He didn't remember much but he did remember how to kiss. Mom fed him lunch. She told the aides he liked juice with his meals and chocolate ice cream for dessert. They got Jim juice and chocolate ice cream.

"How else would they know what he likes?" Mom said.

After lunch, we took Jim to his room. A picture of Mom sat on the night stand next to his bed. Two pairs of pants hung in the closet; socks and underpants were stacked in the dresser; his false teeth sat in a cup on the bathroom shelf.

We stayed two hours. That was enough for all of us. When we said our goodbyes, Jim looked sad and confused. And still he smiled.

I drove Mom down to Payson the following week. Jim slept through lunch. It was a hard visit for Mom. She thanked me for taking her.

The drive over and back was good for both of us. We spent nearly four hours together, just the two of us. More one-on-one time than we had ever spent with each other.

Wendy drove Mom to Payson the next week. Jim never woke up. The week after, we decided to take a break. Mom and I stayed in Sedona. We went to lunch at a Thai restaurant just down the street from Sedona Winds. As I helped Mom out of my car into her wheelchair, my cell phone rang. I looked at the caller ID. It was the Rim Rock Retirement Home. I told Mom it was a client, and let it ring. I wheeled her into the restaurant. I got her settled into a seat and told her I had to call my client. I walked outside the restaurant.

I listened to the message from Rim Rock. It was Shelley, the nurse in charge of Jim's unit. She wanted me to call her.

I reached the receptionist. "Hello, this is Burt Gershater, may I please speak to Shelley in the Behavioral Unit?" A few moments passed.

"Hello, Mr. Gershater," Shelley said. "I wanted you to know that when we took Jim to lunch today, he sat back in his chair and took his last breath."

"Thank you, Shelley."

"I am sorry for your loss," she said.

I told her it was time. She agreed.

"Someone will be down to pick up his belongings," I said.

"There is no hurry, we'll keep them here for you."

I went back in the restaurant.

"Who was it?"

"Just a client," I said.

Mom ordered tempura shrimp and vegetables. I ordered Pad Thai with chicken. We talked a little about Jim, and caught up on the past week.

I had lost my appetite, but I did my best to hold up my end of the conversation. We finally finished our meal, paid the check and I got us loaded into the car.

I drove towards the back of the parking lot, faced a spectacular red rock spire and parked. I looked over at Mom. "Jim died earlier this morning," I said. "They called from Rim Rock just before lunch." I held her hand.

She cried. A cry of sadness. A cry of relief. "He was good to me," she said. "He was ready to go." We sat in the parking lot, looking up at the red rocks.

Mom called the next day. "After you dropped me off, I got a call from the mortuary in Payson. They asked me what I wanted to do with the body.

I told them, cremation. They wanted $1,500!"
I listened.
She said, "$1,500? That's too much, I can get a better price."
I waited.
Mom asked me to call a few mortuaries and get their prices.
"Sure, Mom," I said. I hung up, called around and found one for $750.

I let her know. She called back the Payson Mortuary. They dropped their price.

Mom misses Jim, but it was time for him to go. She got an electric cart last week from Medicare. She really couldn't get around on her walker anymore.

I'm glad she decided to move to Arizona.

# PROTECT WHAT IS PRECIOUS

I don't hear or read the word "precious" much these days. Occasionally I hear it when someone is speaking about a newborn baby or an expensive stone. "Precious" means "valuable". I figure if something is valuable, we should protect it.

Your health is precious. Your mate is precious. Solitude is precious. Art is precious. Peace of mind is precious. Freedom is precious. Sleep is precious. Children are precious. Our earth is precious.

I am precious.

And you are precious.

It's our responsibility to protect what's precious.

## RELIGIOUS HISTORY

Grandma Witia and Grandpa Boris fled Russia at the turn of the century. Jews were under attack. Historically Jews were often blamed for the economic and social ills of a nation. In southern Russia, organized riots targeted Jewish communities; during Passover 1903, innocent Jews were slaughtered.

Jews, like they had done for thousands of years, fled to countries where they wouldn't be persecuted. Grandpa Boris booked passage to the United States in June, 1904 and promised Witia he would send for her and the two girls, Belle and Sara, as soon as he saved enough money.

He arrived in America on June 22, 1904, with only a few dollars, a small suitcase and the clothes he was wearing. He found work in a dry goods store, and two years later sent three tickets for Witia, Belle and Sara to sail to America. They arrived in Philadelphia on June 1906--dazed but free.

Boris and Witia left most of their worldly possessions in Russia--but their Jewish traditions came with them. Judaism illuminated every corner of their lives. Only kosher food was served in their home. They kept two sets of dishes; one for dairy, one nondairy. A mezuzah hung at their front door, reminding all who passed to keep God's word in their minds and hearts. They honored the Sabbath, almost to the letter of the law. They lit candles, recited ancient prayers, and suspended most worldly life from sundown Friday to sundown Saturday. (Not all worldly activity was suspended. Grandpa Boris opened his jewelry store every Saturday morning.)

Grandma and Grandpa stayed faithful to the traditions the rest of their lives. Six more children blessed their home. A century after Grandpa Boris and Grandma Witia arrived in America, their three surviving children--my mother, Aunt Ruthie and Aunt Leah--still reminisce about the celebrations and feasts. They tell heart-warming stories of Grandma's juicy pot roasts, sweet and sour stuffed cabbage, delectable poppy seed cookies and breakfast blintzes.

Grandma and Grandpa were "Keepers of the Faith". They carried the flame of Jewish tradition across the ocean, because it was

what they knew--and it was God's will. They took for granted that
the flame would pass to their children and their children's children.

But in the passing, the flame was altered. As the next generation, my parents, grew up and left home, they focused more on their
careers and families than on traditional Jewish ways.

Soon after I was born, my parents left New York City for the
suburbs and a new life. The second commandment reads: Remember the Sabbath and keep it holy. Twenty-four hours devoted to only
spiritual matters. As I mentioned, Boris and particularly Witia, honored the second Commandment. Not so for my parents.

We didn't light candles on Friday night. We didn't attend
Shabbat services. All my Little League games were played on Saturday mornings. There was no prayer. Kosher laws were ignored.
We loved pork chops, bacon, ham, breakfast sausage, lobster and
shrimp. When Grandma visited, we discretely hid the evidence of
our straying in the rear of the refrigerator.

We became Reformed Jews. Most of the Talmudic laws that
regulated the lives of my ancestors became artifacts. We did attend
services on the holiest days of the year, Rosh Hashanah and Yom
Kippur. My brother and I attended Hebrew School and when we
turned thirteen, celebrated our Bar Mitzvahs. The family gathered
at Aunt Sara and Uncle Leo's every Passover. We ate matzo, bitter herbs, drank four cups of wine, and asked the traditional Four
Questions in Hebrew.

We were Jewish, if not in daily practice, unquestionably in
the spirit of my parent's actions. Doing good deeds, mitzvot, was
for them at the core of being Jewish. My father, a successful ortho-
dontist, volunteered four hours a week at The Pleasantville Cottage
School, a residential home for emotionally disturbed Jewish children. He spent many hours customizing orthodontic appliances for
these challenging young patients. Misshapen mouths were transformed. He performed miracles every Wednesday.

My mother volunteered much of her free time to Haddassah
and B'nai Brith, groups that raised money for Israel. Her sister Leah
emigrated to the Holy Land in 1934. My mom's heart was always
in Israel too. She traveled there every few years and returned home
filled with a joy she never could find in America.

My generation burned for anything but tradition. We grew up
in the 60's. Rebellion was the new rule. "Question Authority" was

pasted on the bumper of every Volkswagen van. We questioned everything: our educational system, the war in Viet Nam, monogamy. Catholics questioned the Pope. We wondered if God was dead. We smoked dope, dropped acid, read Allen Watts, Ram Das, Maharishi and the Dalai Lama. We screamed out for a reality that spoke to us. Reciting lifeless words and singing meaningless songs did not and we were not going to pretend they did. Grandma and Grandpa's ways became irrelevant.

Now, forty years later, I've circled back. The flame of Judaism burns bright. There is a mezuzah at my front and back door. We fast on Yom Kippur and evaluate our lives to set a truer course for the year ahead.

We light Hanukah candles every winter and recount the story of Judah Maccabee defeating the evil King Antiochus in his effort to destroy our people. We hand out chocolate Hanukah gelt and eat potato latkes with applesauce and sour cream.

In the spring, my dear friend Fred Dorfman and I preside over the Passover Seder. Thirty family members and friends crowd into our living room and we tell the story of how God freed the Jews from slavery under Pharaoh. Our service isn't exactly like Uncle Leo's, but the story is the same. I always thank Grandma and Grandpa, my mother and father, and Aunt Sara and Uncle Leo for keeping the tradition; for keeping our story alive.

I make the matzo ball soup as Aunt Sara did. Fred's wife, Audrey, makes the charosis (finely chopped apples, raisins and nuts). Fred grates horseradish root into an industrial strength moror, the bitter herbs reminding us of the harshness of our common path.

But it is not the horseradish or the bitter history that brings the tears to my children's eyes. Their faces shine with joy as they look at me and say, "Thanks, Dad for keeping the torch lit."

Postscript: This past year, I have been studying with a young Chabad rabbi. My knowledge and appreciation of my Jewish roots are deepening. Rabbi Dovi has taught me how to put on tefillan (boxes with Bilblical writings placed inside) and to say the traditional morning prayers. Sabbath has become a day of rest and study, and I have begun to adhere to some of the kosher laws.

These are all things I never dreamt of doing. Today I feel blessed to have returned to these practices which remind me to live each day with truth, love, courage, compassion and purpose.

This has been the best year of my life.

## HOLY VIRGIN MARY

I drove home from Santa Fe, New Mexico with a statue of the Virgin Mary in the back of my red Jeep Grand Cherokee. I bought Her at the flea market. I wasn't looking for the Virgin Mary. I was looking for a statue of St. Francis, but the only St. Francis had a scowl--and a clay bird missing from his left arm.

That morning at the flea market, my friend Kenny and I ambled past booths selling psychedelic T-shirts, organic buffalo jerky, New Age flute music, and rainbows of salsa. Nothing caught my eye. We wandered to the fringe of the fairground. Mexican vendors sold ollas, fresh tortillas, and used car parts out of old pickup trucks and the trunks of their faded sedans. My eye was caught by a majestic statue of the Blessed Mother standing behind a weathered green pickup.

An old man relaxed in a lawn chair next to the truck.

"Señor, how much is the Virgin Mary?"

"No hablo ingles." He called to his son to translate.

I repeated my question.

"A hundred and fifty dollars," the son said.

"Too much."

It was a chilly autumn morning. Business was slow. After a few seconds of silence, the son said, "How much will you give?"

"Seventy-five."

He winced, wrinkled up his nose, scanned the thin crowd of Sunday morning shoppers, and finally shook his head. "Okay."

I gave him the cash. We shook hands. I carefully picked up the statue and held her close to my heart.

Kenny and I and the Blessed Mother headed back to my Jeep. As I held her, I felt a peace I hadn't felt for awhile. It all seemed a little strange to me. A Bar Mitzvah boy. My family scoffed at the story of the Virgin Birth. It was a fairy tale for idiots and yet, this morning, my arms wrapped around Her statue, I felt her gentle love.

I needed comfort. I was driving myself crazy. I had been driving myself crazy for five days after a phone call during which my wife Wendy said something that triggered me. (In my first marriage of twenty-two years, mutual betrayal had been a crippling issue for both of us.)

Though I had been married to Wendy for five years, the wounds of betrayal were still fresh. It didn't take much to trigger the terror of infidelity. Whatever Wendy had said during that call had evoked demons. Cold sweats. Images of Wendy with a former lover. I trusted her without question.

Still, the nightmare played nonstop. (Over the years I had tried nearly everything to find relief from my jealousy. I took antidepressants, but they weakened my sex drive and only made things worse. Counseling gave me limited relief. I took yoga classes. Pushed myself to exhaustion on the treadmill. Nothing stopped the horror movies.)

On that trip to Santa Fe, I was surrounded by friends--good food, good talk, good company. And still I was mostly in a world of my own, piecing together nonexistent evidence, certain my marriage was unraveling. When we gathered around the table for food, wine and laughter, I joined them in body only. I hardly ate. And laughter, usually my refuge, was hard to find.

Kenny, the Holy Mother and I arrived at my Jeep. I wrapped Her in my down sleeping bag and foam mattress, and tucked Her in the back. Kenny and I drove to the airport, where Kenny was catching his flight back to Fresno. We hugged goodbye. I watched him walk away. And then, I was alone with my runaway mind.

I drove home filled with peace and terror. The glow from the Holy Mother calmed my heart, but the fear of marital betrayal never completely left my brain.

Five hours later, I turned down our street. Wendy's car was in the driveway. I pulled in. I was shaking. This was the moment of truth.

Wendy ran out of the house as I walked towards the front door. She wrapped her arms around my neck, kissed me at least a hundred times and led me upstairs to the bedroom.

That evening, I introduced Wendy to the Holy Mother. She liked Her right away. We made a place for Her on the patio nestled close to the rose bushes.

I never told Wendy what had happened in Santa Fe.

## LALO SOMORA

"I'm scared Lalo. I don't want to go."

"We can make it, Edith. I'll hold you."

The Rio Bravo was flowing fast. It was twenty-five yards to the sandy bank on the other side. The water was chest high at the popular and dangerous crossing near Yuma, where Mexicans crossed the border to the United States.

Maybe Edith Madrigal was too scared to cross the Rio Bravo that day. Or maybe she never intended to go with Lalo Samora. Lalo was swept downstream and drowned as Edith watched from the river bank. Only Edith knows what really happened.

Stories come to me. Joyful stories. Tragic stories. Puzzling stories. Heroic stories. This story came to me from the lips of a man who worked at Paseo Stoneworks in Flagstaff, Arizona--Ricardo Rodriquez, a Mexican national working legally in the United States. He was Lalo Samora's best friend.

Ricardo and I met for dinner at Fiesta Burrito. He told me the story of Lalo's life and death:

Lalo Samora grew up in San Pablo de Rancho Grande, a small town in the state of Zacatecas, in north-central Mexico. His father owned farm land and his mother taught high school. Lalo worked all his life: in the fields, in the orange groves, at the car wash.

Lalo was making only ten dollars a day as an automobile mechanic when he decided to leave Mexico seven years ago. He left home and headed north across the harsh Sonoran desert to southern Arizona.

Lalo was thirty-nine years old and had been married to Marisella for sixteen years. They had three girls and a little boy. They had been having marital problems for years. After he came to the United States, he never saw his family. Lalo missed them badly, but he told Ricardo many times, "I am afraid I will die crossing back over the border." Like most Mexican immigrants, Lalo had left his country to make more money.

After he crossed the border, Lalo headed to Flagstaff, Arizona, where he worked odd jobs. A friend told him about Paseo Stoneworks, a local company that installs stone paver driveways and patios. Lalo went to the owner and said, "Please, I need work, I can do anything--I just need work." He was hired on the spot.

Lalo started as a laborer, shoveling sand, hauling paver stones and crushed rock. He did whatever was needed. He even moved to Tucson for a year--two hundred and fifty miles south--to help Paseo. He never complained. He made six dollars and fifty cents an hour, lived with crew members in a trailer on the company lot, and sent half of every pay check to Marisella.

In two years Lalo was promoted to foreman. He learned his skills from Ricardo, a master installer who had trained as a chemical engineer in Mexico. Lalo was put in charge of big projects. He ran a crew of four, and his hourly wage increased to twelve dollars. He sent Marisella nearly a thousand dollars every month. And he sent Salena, his oldest daughter, two hundred.

Customers loved him. Paseo loved him. And he loved Paseo. Lalo asked the new owner, Curt Mansfield, to have all his clothes embroidered with the Paseo logo.

Lalo never missed a day's work. And he never took a vacation in seven years.

But Lalo Samora was lonely. Sadness never left him. As the years went on, he no longer considered himself married, though he faithfully sent half his paycheck to Marisella. He went on dates. He had girlfriends.

Ricardo told me Lalo always spent a lot of money on women. Too much money. He took them to dinner. Bought them clothes and telephones. Ricardo would say, "Lalo, you don't need to spend so much on them. They will like you." Lalo didn't listen. Or, he didn't believe.

January, 2005, Lalo got hooked up with Edith Madrigal who was living in Torreon, Mexico. Lalo's friend, Saul, made the connection. Lalo was forty-six. Edith, twenty-four.

Edith called Lalo one evening. They talked. Lalo called her back. There was a spark. They spoke every day, for hours. "I am crazy for her," Lalo told Ricardo.

Lalo sent Edith money. A lot of money. Ten thousand dollars in three months.

"You don't have to spend so much money on a woman," Ricardo said. "She will like you without spending so much money." Lalo just smiled.

Lalo Samora decided he would bring Edith Madrigal to Flagstaff. He called Marisella and told her his plan: he and Edith would live together in an apartment.

Lalo contacted a "coyote" who arranges border crossings. The place and time was set. Lalo would cross into Mexico at Yuma/Algodones. He would then be driven to the river, a few miles east of Algodones. There he would find the "coyote" and Edith Madrigal.

Lalo had never seen his beloved. Only in photos. Pornographic pictures she had sent him. Pictures Ricardo later found as he sorted through Lalo's belongings.

It was noon. Lalo was driven across the border. He met Edith near the river. They embraced. Two men with inner tubes hurried them to the water. In a few minutes Lalo and Edith would be driving north.

Edith balked.

"I'm scared Lalo. I don't want to go."

Lalo put his arm around her, "We can make it, Edith. I will hold you."

The two men were nervous. "We have to go. NOW!"

Edith Madrigal would not go.

Confused, Lalo crossed the river with the two men. When they reached the other side, Lalo looked back. Edith stood on the shoreline. There was a long moment.

Lalo reentered the river. Edith watched. Lalo struggled, lost his footing. Two men fishing on the Mexican side saw Lalo slip. They tried to help. The water was too fast, too deep. Lalo Samora went under.

Next day, Ricardo got a call from the "coyote". The man was nervous. "Have you seen Lalo?"

Ricardo got another call. It was Edith Madrigal asking for travel money to get back home--five hundred dollars.

Lalo's body was recovered eight days later--only after Ricardo pleaded with Mexican officials to search downstream for his friend.

Lalo Samora was finally laid to rest in his home town in Zacatecas the following week.

Paseo held a farewell party at Cafe Ole' in Flagstaff. All his friends were there to say goodbye.

## MORNING PRAYER WALK

Tony Robbins is the most successful motivational speaker of all time. He's a bazillionaire. He owns an island in Fiji. And his own private jet.

I had never liked Tony Robbins. Of course I had never listened to him.

Tony teaches people to walk on burning coals and to increase their annual income tenfold! Or more!! "You can achieve what you believe"..."Unleash the power within!"... "Master every phase of your life."

It was always too show biz for me. Beds of burning coal. Island in Fiji. Private jet. Consultant to world leaders. But really, down deep, I was jealous of Tony Robbins. I'm a motivational speaker, too. As long as I didn't acknowledge the "Emperor", I could reign unchallenged in my own mind.

Recently, Sevak Khalsa, a colleague and one of my best friends, said to me, "I just bought a ten CD set by Tony Robbins. You have to listen to him. He nails it."

Sevak is a brilliant man, especially in matters of consciousness. He has practiced and taught yoga and meditation for over thirty years. For most of that time he has attended sadna, an early morning two-hour Sikh practice of yoga, meditation, chanting and prayer. He has read hundreds of books on consciousness and regularly passes gems from his readings on to me.

More importantly, three years ago he saved my life--not my physical life, but my dying spirit. I'd been tormented by fantasies of my wife with former lovers. These guys were always stronger, better, bigger. She was happier, more satisfied. I was caught in a downward spiral, image after image, self torment after self torment. One day Sevak asked me how I was doing. I told him.

He said, "You are too old to be doing this to yourself."

I agreed.

"Burt," he said, "you have a great big heart but you are blocked to divine energy that enters through the crown, the seventh chakra. Connect to the divine and you will be at peace."

It all sounded a little too New Agey, but I was desperate. Sevak gave me a simple meditation to strengthen my connection with the Divine. I did it everyday. The images and thoughts didn't stop--but I was able to significantly diminish their assault on my suffering spirit.

If Sevak was brilliant about easing my obsession, why not check out Tony Robbins? As a captive audience. In my own car. I often drive to Phoenix--a two-and-a-half hour trip. This time I decided to checked out Tony's Hour of Power.

Tony's voice roared through the speakers. "If you want to be a positive person, you need positive thoughts. If you want positive thoughts, you have to practice. You are what you practice! Turn your dreams into REALITY!"

GO TONY!!

"If you don't have enough time for an Hour of Power," he said, "then do Thirty Minutes to Thrive; if thirty minutes is too much, Fifteen Minutes to Fulfillment." Sounded good to me.

I listened all the way to Phoenix.

Tony spoke of an ancient yogic technique called breath walking--and its power to relax the body and clear the mind. While walking, one takes in four quick, powerful breaths through the nose followed by four quick powerful exhales through the mouth. With the first inhale, touch the thumb and forefinger of each hand; second inhale, touch your thumb and middle finger; third inhale, thumb and ring finger; and fourth, thumb and pinky. Repeat the finger movements for the exhales.

Tony suggested you breathwalk for twenty minutes and spend the rest of the hour in deep gratitude and visualization.

The day after I broke down and listened to Tony, I gave his techniques a shot. I drove up to Buffalo Park, a jogging trail through a meadow at the base of our sacred mountains. I set out. Breathe. Breathe. Breathe. Breathe. Touch. Touch. Touch. Touch. Breathe. Breathe. Breathe. Breathe. Touch. Touch. Touch. Touch. After twenty minutes I felt alive, open and relaxed.

I moved into the western curve of the trail and continued to follow Tony's instructions: "Thank you God for my life. Thank you for each heartbeat and each breath. And for every step I have ever taken and for every one I will get to take. I am thankful for the warm sun on my face, and the sounds of birds singing overhead. For the snow capped mountains. For the tall pine trees and the billowing clouds."

My breath was easy. My step was light. I was awake, fully awake. I went on. "Thank you, Dad. Thank you, Mom. Thank you, Wendy. Thank you Howard, my dear brother."

I saw each of them clearly. Thank you for touching my life and making it richer, teaching me lessons I need for my journey.

Thank you, my children. Thank you, Jennie. Thank you, Mat. Thank you, Jessie. I saw each of them. Tears of joy streamed from my eyes. I was at peace. I walked on. "Thank you, my closest friends. Thank you everyone who has ever hired me."

These days I save room for whomever enters my mind. Thank you, Dr. Howley, my cardiologist; Steve, my mechanic; Mr. Ashe, my seventh grade teacher who believed in me.

Tony guides me as I approach the end of the trail. I visualize what I want in my life and give thanks as though it has already occurred. This trains my mind to create a clear path to my dreams. I am thankful for my completed book. For an open heart. For a successful talk to the hospital staff. For a joyful vacation with my daughter in the Galapagos. I finish with a Divine Light Meditation, a gift from my friend Sevak.

Tony calls it The Hour of Power; I call it my Prayer Walk. In two years, I have only missed about ten times. I do my Prayer Walk behind the wheel of my car, in airplanes on transcontinental flights, on the beach in San Diego, cross-country skiing in the chilly predawn, on my roller blades on a warm June morning. After my appendectomy, I shuffled, breathwalking, past the nurses' station in my gown, and thanked them for taking care of me.

My life is more peaceful now--but not completely.

On any given Prayer Walk, I may be blissing out on images--of my dad and me skiing together through knee deep snow in Vermont; of my brother Howie and me playing catch in soft twilight; of me, alone, reading on the patio--when I am suddenly jolted from my bliss.

Out of the corner of my eye I see two women coming up from behind, moving faster than I am! I pick up the pace! It's not easy to compete and pray at the same time, but I try.

I am losing ground! I can't maintain the lead without jogging. My knees hurt. Jogging is not a option. They are closing the gap, but I am in luck. There is an exercise station ahead! I pull into the station. I get into push-up position.

"Good morning ladies," I gasp.

"Good morning," they reply, without slowing down.

I hold my phony push-up position till they've gone by.

So much for higher consciousness.

Sometimes I Prayer Walk in my neighborhood. There are no exercise stations! Nearly every day, an old man--at least seventy-years old, wearing a backpack--walks to town. His pace is daunting.

When I hear his step behind me, my brain goes from emitting peaceful alpha waves into reptilian alarm.

"Danger, danger. Old man approaching! Speed up!"

"That won't work. I've tried it before. He's too fast."

"Well at least beat him to the next intersection. Then act like you're stretching."

"Great idea. Saved again."

Maybe Tony will come out with a new CD. Maybe I will. One that teaches how to reach one's highest potential--one that teaches a guy how to let women and old men pass him as he does his Morning Prayer Walk.

## LIVING ALONE

I am fifty-eight years old and I have never lived alone.

I lived with my parents until college. For the first two years, the dormitory was home. A "D" in pre-med chemistry ended my hopes for a medical career. Stunned, I joined Volunteers In Service to America (VISTA). I moved into a fixed-up shack in Rapid City, South Dakota with another volunteer.

I returned to college the following September. An eight-by-twenty foot trailer was my new home--and my first opportunity to live alone. Almost immediately, I fell in love. My sweetheart, Mary Lou, and I spent almost every night together.

We married the following summer. For eight years we worked, we camped, we skied, we traveled. Our first daughter, Jennie, was born in 1976, followed by our son, Mathew, in '78 and another daughter, Jessie, in '82. Solitude never happened. Not mine. Not anyone else's.

After twenty-two years, our marriage ended. Almost immediately I fell in love with Wendy, an old friend. We lived in her apartment when my children went to their mother's. Wendy and I married two years later.

I am fifty-eight years old now, and I haven't slept alone more than fifty-eight nights. That was about to change.

I was in Israel. I called Wendy on her cell. She answered from Bellingham, Washington. Her sister, Susan, had fallen terribly ill. Wendy had flown to be by her side. Susan had been delirious with pneumonia when she finally checked into the hospital.

As Wendy and the family kept watch, Susan's condition deteriorated. Septic shock, a life-threatening bacterial infection, set in. Body tissues and organs were cut off from their oxygen supply. Susan didn't respond to treatment. She developed Acute Respiratory Distress Syndrome (ARDS), a deadly lung disorder. Her breathing faltered. The doctors put her on a ventilator and heavily sedated her. Susan retained seventy pounds of fluid; she was so bloated, her skin was translucent.

The family prayed.

A few days later Susan began to breathe on her own. Slowly, the fluid drained from her body.

The family kept vigil.

The doctors told them that when treatment is successful, the patient continues to breathe, and regains mobility. Susan breathed on her own, but she didn't move. A brain scan was ordered. Susan had pervasive brain damage. Susan might never return.

I came back from Israel. Wendy stayed in Washington. Three and a half months went by. Wendy came home and told me she wanted to move to Washington--for a year. She would be close to Susan, and be able to care for Susan's fourteen year old daughter, Natalie. (Natalie's father, Tony, was physically and mentally incapacitated by multiple schlerosis.)

I had been fine with Wendy being gone for three-and-a-half months. A year was too long. My sleep suffered. I tossed and turned all night, wondering if Wendy would ever leave Susan and Natalie. Wendy assured me this separation was temporary. She needed more time. I told her I would do my best.

We had no solid agreement about time. Weary, lonely and afraid, I began to shut down. Our telephone calls got shorter. My voice grew flat. I poked her with my fear: "How can we afford this? You're going to have to kiss Susan goodbye sometime...what are you waiting for? Natalie has family in Bellingham...she'll be okay. Bad things happen to people, but life goes on."

Divorce scenarios crept into my brain. Move into an apartment. See a lawyer. Split the assets. Divide the furniture.

My heart was heavy.

I started to clean the house. The landing area outside the bedroom was a mess. Old Sports Illustrated magazines. Papers we hadn't looked at for years. Bags of God-only-knows what.

An antique sewing machine, we used as a catchall. As I cleared papers off it, I saw a dusty 3 x 5 card with Wendy's handwriting. There were three quotes:

"You'll never be hurt as much by being open
as you have been by remaining closed."

"The meaning of life is not what happens to
people; the meaning of life is what happens
between people."

"Good morning! This is God. I will be handling all
your problems today. I won't need your help--so
have a great day!"

I started crying. I didn't want bitterness to harden my heart. I didn't want to leave Wendy to deal with this tragedy alone. She needed to be with Susan and Natalie, and I had to find a place inside me, a place where alone was okay, where alone was sanctuary, not punishment.

You don't stop a fifty-eight year old habit in fifty-eight seconds. I needed help. I talked with my oldest daughter, Jennie. She knew my conflict.

"Daddy," she said "the last thing Wendy needs is to be wondering if you're going to stay with her. She loves you."

I nodded.

Tears rolled down Jennie's cheeks. "You've never been by yourself, Daddy. This is an opportunity for you to find peace."

Kamila, my Sufi counselor, told me bitterness and divorce were, indeed, options. Bad ones. God was giving me a gift. Kamila spoke of supplication, a humble request for divine assistance. "Your intellect is not enough for this challenge. Ask for help."

The next morning, on my prayer-walk, I asked, "God, please help me." I waited.

The words "become invisible" came to me. "Watch...breathe... become invisible" .

Wendy wasn't leaving me. I was the one leaving. For the first time in fifty-eight years, I would live alone. For the first time in fifty-eight years, I was willing to be with myself.

## BACK IN THE HOLY LAND

"Boker tov." Good morning. "Chag somayach." Happy holidays.

I greeted morning walkers with my rusty Hebrew. I was back in Israel after forty years, strolling the city park in Had HaSharon. "Boker tov." "Chag somayach."

Two weeks prior to my departure, the Israeli military assassinated Sheik Ahmed Yassin, founder of Hamas, a military organization whose sole purpose is to destroy Israel and raise the Palestinian flag over the region. Israel killed Yassin in retaliation for two years of Palestinian suicide bombers killing hundreds of civilian Israelis.

Hamas and other military groups vowed revenge for Yassin's death. TV showed mobs in Gaza and the West Bank shouting "DEATH TO AMERICA!" "DEATH TO ISRAEL!", and tearing apart effigies of President Bush and Prime Minister Sharon.

My wife Wendy asked me to postpone the trip. Wait out the unrest. Friends feared for my safety as they watched the growing violence on the evening news.

I didn't care about my safety. I wanted to be with my Aunt Leah, and cousins Zevi and Nira for Passover.

My Aunt Leah became a committed Zionist in her late teens. She burned to visit the Holy Land. In 1934, a month after her college graduation, she sailed from New York City and arrived in Haifa twenty-five days later, armed only with her courage and a brand new degree in English.

In short order, she met, fell in love with, and married Avshalom Carmeli, a wild young Zionist sabra (a Jew born in The Holy Land). They returned to the United States for their wedding. While they were in the states, WWII broke out in Europe. Germans mined the coastal waters surrounding Europe. Commercial ships stopped sailing the Atlantic. Leah and Avshalom could not go home.

Four years later, in 1945, Leah and Avshalom found a convoy carrying supplies through the blockade. After thirty harrowing days, they arrived in Palestine. Upon arrival, Avshalom worked for the Israeli army and Leah prepared for their first child. In 1946, Zevi was born. Nira arrived two years later, during the Israeli War of Independence.

In 1964, a few days after my high school graduation, I flew to Israel for the summer. Israel had just turned sixteen. I had just turned eighteen. I am not sure why I went to Israel that summer. I had a beautiful girlfriend. I'd forgotten most of the Hebrew I learned in Hebrew School, and I had no interest in my Jewish heritage or Zionism.

I was a jock. I liked fun, and going to Israel seemed like fun. Besides, I had met Leah and Zevi in the U.S. and I wanted to see them again. And I wanted to finally meet Avshalom and Nira.

I was never the same after that trip. I ate hummus, tahini, falafel and pita, and at least ten Greek olives with every meal. I swam in the Dead Sea, stood on the hostile Northern border between Israel and Lebanon, swam in the clear springs of the Ein Gedi oasis, and looked up the towering walls of Masada where, in 73 C.E., nine hundred and sixty Jews chose death by their own hand rather than slavery under the Romans.

I loved my adventures, but they were not the most important part of that summer. What mattered the most that summer was that my Aunt Leah listened to me. She asked thoughtful questions and enjoyed my answers. She was delighted to hear my ideas. We spent hours in conversation. For the first time in my life, I was encouraged to speak. I was invited to explore my ideas. Lay them on the table. No criticism. No judgment. That was the Holy Land for me.

Mornings, I worked in Uncle Avshalom's wholesale produce market, side by side with Chalil, a thirty year old Palestinian. We began work before the sun rose. We lifted boxes laden with fruits and vegetables from the farmers' trucks: green grapes, red grapes, purple grapes, tomatoes, cucumbers, hot peppers, sweet peppers, pears, apples, eggplants, plums, green onions, yellow onions, cantaloupe and watermelons. When we finished unloading the farmers' trucks, we loaded the vendors' trucks for market.

At ten we took a break. Chalil made salad from fresh cucumber, tomato and green onions. He chopped them into small pieces. Squeezed in fresh lemon. Sprinkled salt and pepper and served it from a common bowl with freshly baked pita. It was the best salad I had ever eaten. I still make it today.

Chalil and I mostly spoke to one another by smiling. Boker Tov...we smiled. Stacking produce in the warehouse...we smiled.

Chalil and his family honored my Israeli family and me with a lamb feast at his Arab village...we smiled. At the end of the summer, Chalil gave me a miniature bronze tea set that still sits in my living room. We hugged shalom...and smiled.

Three years later, Chalil was murdered by Palestinians while he herded sheep in the Golan Heights. No one knows who killed him. His throat was slashed and he was left to die.

That summer I was with Zevi or Nira or both of them every day. We traveled to Jerusalem, the Galilee, Haifa, Solomon's Mines. We swam in the Dead Sea. They taught me Hebrew and we squabbled like siblings.

In the years that followed, Leah, Nira and Zevi visited America. Nira came in the early seventies and we celebrated my first Passover away from New York. At that time, nearly ten years had elapsed since my last Seder. Nira refreshed me on the traditions. We created a memorable celebration complete with all the symbols of the holiday.

Zevi came to America many times for business. We always made sure to spend a few days together, usually in Las Vegas. And when Leah came, I always traveled to see her. (Avshalom had died in Israel, a few years after my summer visit).

Israelis ask one question to every Jew they talk to in America. "When are you coming to Israel?" Nira asked me. Leah asked me. Zevi asked me every time we met.

My response was always the same: a guilty smile and a weak promise to visit in the near future. I was too busy. It cost a lot of money. I had three young children in school. It was too dangerous.

They never stopped asking.

In June 2003, Wendy and I met Zevi and his wife Ahuva in Las Vegas. We hugged. We laughed . We ate too much food. We shopped. Went to a show. We strolled the crowded streets, and wandered through the casinos: Bellagio, Mandalay Bay, Paris Las Vegas, The Venetian and Caesar's Palace.

At breakfast on the last day, Zevi looked at me. "When are you coming to Israel? You always say you are coming but you never do."

He was right. I was tired of my lame excuses. "I will come to Israel soon," I said. He didn't believe me, but I knew I would be in the Holy Land within the year.

"Boker tov." "Chag somayach."

I greeted the other walkers in the park. I was breath-walking. I walked. I breathed deeply. I thanked God for my blessings.

I thanked Leah for sailing to Israel seventy years ago. I thanked my mother for keeping the love of Israel alive in our home. I thanked my parents for sending me to Israel forty years ago. I thanked the soldiers who fought and died for our homeland. I thanked Zevi for nudging me to return.

And I thanked Chalil for his friendship.

# PRACTICE SUGGESTIONS

We are all love generators. The amount of love we generate is solely up to us. Creating love is both our choice and our responsibility. It is often the hardest, most unnatural choice available.

I have dedicated this section of the book to suggestions to assist you in living each lesson. I offer four suggestions for each lesson. Why four? It could have been twenty-four. But four is a manageable number. Do one of them. Do it four times. Do all of them. Do two. Do them over and over. Use your own. Invent new ones. The more you practice, the more natural creating love becomes.

It is not enough to know how to create love. We get no points for our knowledge of love. We only get points for participating in its creation.

Love is a verb.

## NOBODY IS PERFECT

**ONE:** Be aware when you are judging others. Judging others is a drug that makes us feel better--for a moment.

Be aware when you judge yourself. Judging yourself is a drug that makes you feel worse--for longer than a moment.

When we judge, we put an end to curiosity and learning.
And remember, judgment is not the same as discernment.

**TWO:** Practice listening. Listening is the best way to find out something new about another person. Listening suspends judgment and we can actually learn something.

**THREE:** Work on your apologies. Remember an apology has two parts: a heart-felt expression of sorrow for your action AND your conscious, disciplined effort to not repeat the offending behavior!

**FOUR:** Always remind yourself "we are all a work-in-progress".
It is only by missing the mark that we learn to reset our sights and improve. "We learn by our mistakes" is not just a saying, it is one of the great truths of life.

## YOUR TEACHERS ARE EVERYWHERE

**ONE:** Call up an old teacher, one who made a difference in your life. Thank her or him and tell them specifically how they touched you. Teachers work hard and they rarely hear from their old students after the final school bell rings at end of the school year.

Make the call before that Final Bell really does ring.

**TWO:** Strike up a conversation with a stranger. Ask them questions about their life. Listen. Ask them more questions. Listen more. Let yourself be filled with the wonder and the wisdom of another person's story.

**THREE:** Listen to your children as if they are teaching you about life. Don't panic, there will be plenty of time for you to teach. Ask them what turns them on. Ask them what turns them off. Just listen. Let your heart be curious. Children only talk to people who are really interested in them.

**FOUR:** Look at yourself in the mirror. Take a full breath. Release it. Take another full breath. Release it. Say these words softly: "I am beautiful." Say them again, "I am beautiful." Pay attention to what you feel. If you are having difficulty saying the words or taking in the message, you have some important work ahead of you.

### YOU ARE BEAUTIFUL!

## HONOR YOUR FRIENDS

**ONE:** Stay in touch with your buddies. If they live close by, get together for a meal. Go to the movies. See a play. Make tamales together. Watch a game on TV. Go for a hike. Nothing fancy, though fancy works too.

If they live far away, get together as much as possible or more. Telephone, e-mail, text, letters. Stay in touch.

**TWO:** Attend important rites of passage: weddings, marriages, Bar Mitzvahs, La Quinceañera, baptisms, graduations, recitals, athletic events, and funerals. If I missed one, fill in the space.

**THREE:** On Veterans Day, call your friends who served in the military. Thank them for their service. If they were in combat, spend a little more time thanking them. They can't get enough thanks for their sacrifices.

**FOUR:** If you believe your friend is making an error in his or her life, let them know. With love. If a friend won't do this, who will?

P. S. If you are the friend being spoken to, listen--and thank your courageous friend for speaking to you.

## COMMITMENT IS NOT A FEELING

**ONE:** Give your money to worthy causes. Give to your church, synagogue or mosque. Give money to homeless people and don't worry that they might not use it wisely. Give no matter how much you earn, give more than you are comfortable giving. It needs to hurt before it feels good.

**TWO:** Transform your burdens into blessings. This is easier said than done, so keep the Serenity Prayer close by:

> *God, grant me the serenity*
> *to accept the things*
> *I cannot change,*
> *the courage to change the things I can,*
> *and the wisdom to know*
> *the difference.*

We are all given challenges. When we think of them as burdens, we become depressed and angry. When we finally accept that we only have two good choices: to change what is or accept what is--we open up room for courage, creativity, joy and love.

**THREE:** Create a regular practice. Write daily. Pray daily. Do yoga. Paint. Practice a martial art. Do it even when you don't feel like doing it. Discipline rarely feels good on the front end. It is only afterwards that you feel the rewards. If we wait to feel good to do good things, good things rarely happen.

**FOUR:** Hire a coach to keep you on track. I never would have finished this book if I hadn't sat down with my editor regularly for over a year. She held me accountable. I wouldn't be running hundred yard dashes in my sixty-second year if I hadn't worked with a trainer to get my old arthritic legs working again. He held me accountable. I would never have gotten my motivational speaking career off the ground without my Small Business Development counselors. They held me accountable. Hire a coach! Hire more than one. You are worth it.

## PROTECT WHAT IS PRECIOUS

**ONE:** Nothing should be taken for granted. Spend time in gratitude for your uncountable blessings: air to breathe, water to drink, the sun's warmth, the sun's light, your children, your wife, your parents, your employer, every blade of grass, every grain of sand, snow to ski on--or to shovel. There is no end to this list.

My friend Sevak told me, "If you were grateful for every breath, it would not be too much."

**TWO:** Tell stories when you gather. Tell the story of Moses leading the Jews out of slavery. Tell the story of the Sermon on the Mount. Tell about Buddha--just sitting. Talk about Martin Luther King and Harriet Tubman leading their people to freedom. Gandhi. The Dalai Lama. Winston Churchill. Jackie Robinson. Susan B. Anthony. Joan of Arc.

Tell stories about your personal heroes: your mom, your dad, your seventh grade teacher, your son, and your daughter. Your friend who...Your partner who...By telling stories we keep them alive. Keep them alive!

**THREE:** Say grace before meals. Silently. Out loud. Head bowed. Looking up, looking around the table--looking inward. Say an old standard or make up a new one. For a few seconds or a few minutes. There are no rules for grace. It simply is.

**FOUR:** Take time alone. Just you. No computer. No TV. No cell phone. No music. No kids. No shopping. No driving.

Walking is good. Sitting--just sitting. Your spirit is holy. It needs quiet.

# EPILOGUE

I was the guy who never shared an emotion until he was thirty years old.

I was the guy who hid behind the double walls of "aloof" and "funny".

I was the guy who couldn't ask for anything--and seethed when my unspoken desires went unmet.

I was the guy who would interpret rejection in every interaction.

I was the guy who needed to judge somebody--anybody--in order to feel a little better about himself.

I was the guy who unmercifully judged himself, especially in the dark hours of the night.

I was the guy who could never accept a compliment.

I was the guy who also didn't give them out.

I was the guy who never acknowledged his God-given talents.

And I was the guy who abused his beautiful son.

I was that guy.

I am not that guy today. Not even close.

I always knew I had a warm heart. What I didn't know was how afraid I was to expose it. At some point in my life, I chose love over fear.

Maybe it happened at Esalen Institute at age twenty-eight. Maybe it happened during the ten years of group therapy. Maybe it happened when I nearly lost my son's trust. It rarely came as a jolt of Divine wisdom (although it happened that way too). It was mostly more incremental. A step at a time.

I chose to expose my guts to the world. I chose to expose my heart. I chose to ask for what I needed. I noticed how much I judged everyone (especially me) and started doing it less. I stopped taking everything personally. I began to accept compliments and give them out. I slowly understood the gifts God gave me.

I stopped hurting my son.

I stopped hurting myself.

I have been blessed. Blessed to live long enough to start a new chapter. Blessed to find teachers (they are everywhere). Blessed to peel off layers of fear. Blessed to find my courage. And infinitely blessed to be surrounded with love.

I hope my stories touched you deeply. May they awaken your courage to make love the center of your life.

Burt Gershater is the author of two books:
*No Guts No Love* and *Poems From His Heart*

For information and to order:
www.burtgershater.com

or

Sacred Pages Publishing
222 North Verde Street
Flagstaff, AZ 86001
928-774-6400

Burt is available for speaking
engagements and training seminars.
www.burtgershater.com